THE BIBLE TELLS ME SO

THE BIBLE TELLS ME SO

WHY DEFENDING SCRIPTURE
HAS MADE US UNABLE TO READ IT

PETER ENNS

HarperOne

An Imprint of HarperCollinsPublishers

HarperOne

THE BIBLE TELLS ME SO: *Why Defending Scripture Has Made Us Unable to Read It.* Copyright © 2014 by Peter Enns. All rights reserved. Printed in the United States of America. No part of this book may be used or reproduced in any manner whatsoever without written permission except in the case of brief quotations embodied in critical articles and reviews. For information address HarperCollins Publishers, 195 Broadway, New York, NY 10007.

HarperCollins books may be purchased for educational, business, or sales promotional use. For information please e-mail the Special Markets Department at SPsales@harpercollins.com.

HarperCollins website: http://www.harpercollins.com

HarperCollins®, 📖®, and HarperOne™ are trademarks of HarperCollins Publishers.

FIRST HARPERCOLLINS PAPERBACK EDITION PUBLISHED IN 2015

Designed by Matthew Van Zomeren
Maps by Beehive Mapping

Library of Congress Cataloging-in-Publication Data

Enns, Peter
The Bible tells me so : why defending scripture has made us unable to read it / Peter Enns. — First Edition.
pages cm
Includes bibliographical references.
ISBN 978-0-06-227203-4
1. Bible--Criticism, interpretation, etc. I. Title.
BS511.3.E56 2014
220.1—dc23
2014010141

23 24 25 26 27 LBC 18 17 16 15 14

To seekers and pilgrims who need to think out loud,
others who would like to,
and those who value and support them.

*   *   *

And to my family—already and not yet.

Concerning the Bible . . .

"The human qualities of the raw materials show through. Naïvety, error, contradiction, even (as in the cursing Psalms) wickedness are not removed. The total result is not 'the Word of God' in the sense that every passage, in itself, gives impeccable science or history. It carries the Word of God; and we (under grace, with attention to tradition and to interpreters wiser than ourselves, and with the use of such intelligence and learning as we may have) receive that word from it not by using it as an encyclopedia or an encyclical but by steeping ourselves in its tone or temper and so learning its overall message."

*   *   *

"We might have expected, we may think we should have preferred, an unrefracted light giving us ultimate truth in systematic form—something we could have tabulated and memorized and relied on like the multiplication table. . . . But there is one argument which we should beware of using . . .:

God must have done what is best, this is best, therefore God has done this. For we are mortals and do not know what is best for us, and it is dangerous to prescribe what God must have done—especially when we cannot, for the life of us, see that He has after all done it."

C. S. Lewis, *Reflections on the Psalms*

Contents

Author's Note

A WORD ABOUT how this book is laid out.

I refer to the Bible a lot, and almost all of the citations (chapter and verse) are collected toward the end of the book in an easy-to-use section, "Where in the Bible Were We? (In Order of Appearance)." I assume you're as distracted as I am when you're reading along in a book, having a good time, and you come across something like "(Isaiah 58:9–10; Luke 4:10; John 12:1–3, 7–11, and 15)" and you stop dead in your tracks, wondering "Where did the words go?" So I collected all that in the back of the book. You'll also find in that section a few references to other books and articles I used as sources.

It's hard to talk about the Bible without dates, so you'll notice a few popping up here and there. I've kept them to a minimum and collected them at the end of the book in a crisp and clear timeline, "Some Dates I Keep Referring To (And a Few Others)." You'll also find at the end a list of books that you might find helpful if you want to keep reading a bit ("In Case You Don't Believe Me and Want to Read More").

The Bible translation I use throughout the book is the *New Revised Standard Version*. Just because. I like it.

I'll Take Door Number Three

When the Bible Doesn't Behave

THE BIBLE.

It's been around in one form or another for twenty-five hundred years or so, and, by anyone's standards, it's had quite a run.

From its murky beginnings as ancient stories and poems written by obscure peoples living along the eastern Mediterranean coast in a plot of land the size of New Jersey, it became a worldwide sacred and revered text, the Holy Bible, the Word of God, read in hundreds of languages and dialects, the number one bestselling book of all time, with billions of copies sold and a hundred million more sold each year.

The Bible isn't going anywhere. Christians have been reading it ever since there have been Christians. It remains *the* main way for Christians today to learn about God, the go-to sourcebook for spiritual comfort, guidance, and insight.

Count me among them. I am a Christian, and the Bible has shaped and continues to shape my life and my faith. I love the Bible, because I meet God in its pages. I teach the Bible because I want to help others meet God, too.

So what's the problem?

Many Christians have been taught that the Bible is Truth downloaded from heaven, God's rulebook, a heavenly instructional manual—follow the directions and out pops a true believer; deviate from the script and God will come crashing down on you with full force.

If anyone challenges this view, the faithful are taught to "defend the Bible" against these anti-God attacks. Problem solved.

That is, until you actually read the Bible. Then you see that this rulebook view of the Bible is like a knockoff Chanel handbag—fine as long as it's kept at a distance, away from curious and probing eyes.

What I discovered, and what I want to pass along to you in this book, is that this view of the Bible does not come from the Bible but from an anxiety over protecting the Bible and so regulating the faith of those who read it.

Why do I say this? The Bible tells me so.

I will tell you my story soon, but in sum I would say this: When you read the Bible on its own terms, you discover that it doesn't behave itself like a holy rulebook should. It is definitely inspiring and uplifting—it wouldn't have the shelf life it does otherwise. But just as often it's a challenging book that leaves you with more questions than answers.

For one thing, you don't have to go beyond the first two books of the Bible, Genesis and Exodus, to find stories that are hard to take at face value and read more like scripts for a fairy tale.

Adam and Eve, the two first humans, live in a garden paradise with not one but two magical trees, and lurking nearby is a talking serpent with an ax to grind. God shows up on a semiregular basis and chats with humans—as if, what could be more normal? A sea parts down the middle so Israelite slaves can escape Egypt on dry land. Fire comes out of the sky. God slays sea monsters.

Christians know deep down that these stories, as part of the Holy Bible, need to be taken seriously. But still. If we read these sorts of episodes outside of the Bible, from another ancient culture, we wouldn't blink an eye. We'd know right away we were dealing with the kinds of stories people wrote long ago and far away, not things that happened, and certainly nothing to invest too much of ourselves in.

Yet this stuff is in the Bible, the *Holy* Bible, the book that we are told gives the faithful sure spiritual guidance and relays absolutely reliable information about God. It's not supposed to feel like Norse sagas or the SyFy Channel.

So what are we supposed to do with a Bible like this?

Another challenging part for Christian readers who see the Bible as an unerring rulebook is the many laws God gave the Israelites on Mount Sinai (with Moses as the go-between). These laws are at the heart and center of Israel's story, the Old Testament,* which makes up three-fourths of the Christian Bible.

But for Christians many of these laws are completely out of touch with their day-to-day spiritual reality, and it's hard to know whether we should take them seriously or move along without making eye contact.

Animals are sacrificed on a regular basis to appease God, with very specific instructions given by God about what kind of animals and when to sacrifice them to keep him† calm. Other laws are just plain weird. Wet dreams, contact with mold and bodily discharges, and eating pork, dolphin, and lobster make you "unclean," an ancient notion about being unfit to be in the company of God and fellow Israelites. The blind, disfigured, hunchbacked, dwarfed, and those with crushed testicles (I suppose it could happen) are barred from the priesthood. Strictly speaking, the Americans with Disabilities Act is unbiblical.

There's a reason pastors' sermons and Bible study groups don't spend a lot of time in these sections: it's hard to know what to do with all this, and there doesn't seem to be a lot of payoff in investing the effort to try.

Other parts of the Bible are shocking to read, even barbaric, and hard

---

* I will use the conventional Christian term "Old Testament" when talking about the sacred writings of the ancient Israelites—a.k.a. the Hebrew Bible or Tanakh, an acronym for the three sections of the Jewish Bible, Torah (five books of Moses), Nevi'im (prophets), and Kethuvim (writings).

† I do not believe that the God of the universe is male or female, but, following the biblical convention, I will use male pronouns when speaking of God. We will be looking at a lot of passages from the Bible, and adjusting the language at each point could get distracting and become the unintended focus. I realize—and respect—that not all would agree with me in this decision, but I just want to be clear about what I am doing and why.

to defend as the Word of God in civil adult conversation. God either orders a lot of killing or does it himself—and even comes across as a bit touchy. You only have to get to the sixth chapter of the Bible to see God drown all but two of every living creature on earth in a forty-day tsunami because humanity was wicked and evil (except for Noah). Later God drowned (what is it with water?) the entire Egyptian army in the Red Sea after the Israelites passed through safely.

Then (as we'll see in the next chapter), to take occupation of their new homeland, the land of Canaan—the Promised Land—God commanded the Israelites to go from town to town and exterminate the current residents—men, women, children, and animals—and move in. If we read this anywhere else, we would call it genocide. Later, for much of Israel's history, warfare with other nations was as common as football in October, and defeating Israel's enemies wasn't a necessary evil but brought God glory and honor. And when provoked, God wasn't bashful about killing or plaguing his own people. The God of the universe often comes across like a tribal warlord.

All this is part of the Christian Bible that Christians are often taught to take without question as God speaking to them.

What are we supposed to *do* with a Bible like this?

What are we supposed to do with a *God* like this?

*   *   *

Taking the Bible seriously enough to read it carefully, as many Christians can testify to, can generate more than its share of uh-oh moments. The Bible can become a challenge *to* one's faith in God rather than the source of faith, a problem to be overcome rather than the answer to our problems.

The Holy Bible, the sourcebook for spiritual comfort, guidance, and insight, makes you squirm—or at least fidget. It just won't do to make believe otherwise. In fact, it's good to come clean about it and clear the air. The question is what to do about it.

The Bible Isn't the Problem

CHRISTIANS WHO LOOK to the entire Bible as God's Word, and so take the time and effort to respect the Bible enough to read it carefully, often find their faith deeply challenged—even stretched to the breaking point. Feeling like you are losing your handle on your faith and on God produces stress.

No one likes stress. We want to get rid of it, or at least take it down a few notches. To cope we often ignore or push down the stress and go along with life on autopilot, acting as if everything is okay. But "keeping it together" uses up a lot of energy and eventually takes its toll.

Think of a relationship where something is clearly not right, but facing the problem is too emotionally risky. We come up with all sorts of ways to convince ourselves that so-and-so really *is* a thoughtful sweetheart deep down and *not* a narcissistic sarcastic dipwad. Holding on tooth and nail to something that's not working, denying that nagging undercurrent of tension, that feeling that you *know* something's just not right, and just going on with life—well, that's hard, stressful work.

Plus, stress erodes basic people skills we learned in kindergarten. It makes us edgy, angry, nasty, and passive-aggressive. We kick the dog, yell at the kids, and make ourselves and those around us miserable.

I know many Christians who deal with this stress every day—sometimes they don't even know it's happening until some unexpected experience snaps them out of the stupor and connects them with their heart. I've been there. Sometimes I still am.

The real shame is that it's hard to talk about Bible-induced stress with the very people you'd think you should be able to talk to—religious leaders, teachers, and church friends. It's risky to let them in on your little secret, what you're really thinking, because you're afraid they'll look at you like you have a massive zit on your nose. Or worse, you'll be scolded like a misbehaved child or shamed and shunned for your faithlessness.

And for good reason: we have all heard of stories where people have become casualties for asking questions about scripture. So, you go it alone, doomed to a lifelong sound track of nagging doubt and stress, or you just leave your faith on the curbside with the rest of the week's trash.

And now for some good news: I believe God wants us to take the Bible seriously, but I don't believe he wants us to suppress our questions about it.

I don't believe he wants us to be in constant crisis, in a stress-reduction mode of having to smooth over mass floods, talking animals, or genocide.

I don't believe God wants us to live our lives wringing our hands over how to make the Bible behave itself, expending energy 24/7 to make the Bible into something it's not, and calling that "serving God."

The problem isn't the Bible.

The problem is coming to the Bible with expectations it's not set up to bear.

If we come to the Bible expecting something like a spiritual owner's manual complete with handy index, a step-by-step field guide to the life of faith, an absolutely sure answer-book to unlock the mystery of God and the meaning of life, then conflict and stress follow right behind and, like a leech, find a place in your heart and soul to latch on.

When we are taught that the Bible *has* to meet these unrealistic expectations for our faith to be genuine, the end product is a fragile, nervous faith. Faith like that produces stress, because it has to be tended and defended with 24/7 vigilance in order to survive—like an abandoned baby robin in a shoebox. And even with constant tending, it still may not survive.

Is a life of faith in God truly *supposed* to be this stressful? Is this what God wants for us? I don't think so. So let's stop making it that way by setting the Bible up to be something it's not prepared to be and then anxiously smoothing over the rough parts to make it fit false expectations. The cost is too high.

So here's my not so radical thought: What if the Bible is just fine the way it is? What if it doesn't need to be protected from itself? What if it doesn't need to be bathed and perfumed before going out in public?

And what if *God* is actually fine with the Bible just as it is without needing anyone to stand guard over it? Not the well-behaved-everything-is-in-order version we create, but the messy, troubling, weird, and ancient Bible that we actually have?

Maybe *this* Bible has something to show us about our own sacred journey of faith, and maybe God wants us to wander off the beach blanket to discover what that is.

Sweating bullets to line up the Bible with our exhausting expectations, to make the Bible something it's not meant to be, isn't a pious act of faith, even if it looks that way on the surface. It's actually thinly masked fear of losing control and certainty, a mirror of an inner disquiet, a warning signal that deep down we do not really trust God at all.

A Bible like that isn't a sure foundation of faith but a barrier to true faith. Creating a Bible that behaves itself doesn't support the spiritual journey. It cripples it.

The Bible just as it is isn't a problem to be fixed. It's an invitation.

My Life, in Brief, and Such as It Is

I'VE BEEN ON A JOURNEY of rediscovering the Bible and the God behind it for over thirty years and I don't see that journey ending any time soon.

Parts of my journey are specific to people like me who "do Bible" for a living, though I'd bet good money (I'm a professor, so let's start the bidding low) that my story will ring a bell for others—whether you are Christian, used to be, are on the way out, or are thinking about it but can't get over the Bible hump.

My parents were German immigrants, straight out of central casting, who settled in New Jersey and raised me to know God in a genuine but European "don't let it get out of hand" sort of way. They sent me to two years of Lutheran confirmation classes during junior high school, but not a lot of it stuck at the time—though the cross I received as a gift at my confirmation now hangs on my study wall.

My religiously benign childhood took a more dramatic turn one Sunday while in high school. I found myself in an evangelistic church service, where I "raised my hand and went forward" because "If I died tonight," I was pretty sure I was headed straight to hell, and raising my hand, apparently, was what I needed to do to keep that from happening. For the next couple of years I alternated between imposing that same terror on my friends (with little effect) and acting cool and all high-schooly, as if nothing had happened.

I wound up at a small evangelical Christian college a few hours from home. I wanted to find someplace where I could grow in my faith, but I wound up spending most of my time trying to get this girl to like me (eventually successful—I married her) and trying to locate my fastball (very unsuccessful—I hold the school record for wild pitches). My faith was on autopilot.

Things began to change the fall after graduation. It was a November morning in 1982, and as I was taking a walk, deep in prayer, in a trance, in my third day of fasting, and having just given all my worldly possessions to the poor, I looked up and, behold, a great light, and a voice spoketh forth unto me saying. . . .

Not quite. God met me in a mundane and unexpected moment.

I attended my high school Thanksgiving homecoming football game with an old friend. He had also graduated from a Christian college, but unlike me he learned something. In the parking lot we ran into an old classmate, an atheist, smart as a whip, with a degree in philosophy.

We talked for a bit and, for some reason I can't recall, the topic turned to Christianity. Both my friends—the smart atheist and the smart Christian—were going at it like it was the Lincoln-Douglas debates. I stood there, an idiot in the middle of something clearly over my head, acting like I was tracking deeply but just choosing to be silent.

Funny how things happen, but that brief chance conversation with friends changed the course of my life. It hit me that I knew *nothing* about what I said I believed—and that after going to a Christian college with all the mandatory Bible classes, chapel services, and same-sex dorms.

To sum up, I felt stupid and humiliated.

I had come to Turning Point Number 1.

Right then and there, feeling ashamed for being so utterly dumb about my faith, I vowed, "If I'm going to do this Jesus thing, I'm going to know what I'm talking about." It's not always the best idea to begin your spiritual quest driven by shame and a desire for intellectual power, but if that's what it takes, so be it. And like I said, God tends to meet us where we are—in my case, throwing an intellectual temper tantrum.

I had no idea what I was in for, but such is the bliss of ignorant (and arrogant) youth.

I started reading. I read the Bible cover to cover several times over the next three years along with books about the Bible. I read books on theology, church history, philosophy, and anything else I could find, with a dictionary always close by. I also got to know a new friend, C. S. Lewis, and read for the first time his beloved children's books *The Chronicles of Narnia*—as a twenty-two-year-old, sitting on my childhood bed, an apt metaphor for my spiritual state.

I don't remember exactly when, but one day it dawned on me that I was becoming . . . a reader—and that distant thud you just heard was the sound of the fainting bodies of everyone who ever knew me. And not just a reader, but the reclusive "I'm fine not showering just leave me alone I'm reading" sort of reader. Not bad for a guy whose youth consisted mainly of sports and *Gilligan's Island* reruns. I had read voluntarily a grand total of one book in junior high school (*The Chosen*), another one in high school (*Dracula*), and two more in college (I don't remember). Now I couldn't stop. I think my friends may have tried an intervention.

I suppose the next step was inevitable. Three years out of college I left the world of the living and went to seminary, a conservative but sane Calvinist (Presbyterian) seminary my pastor recommended. I was never interested in training to become a pastor, and frankly I cannot imagine a worse plight upon the Christian world. I was there for a higher and more noble purpose: to figure things out, such as God, Jesus, the Bible, my faith, the meaning of life, time-space continuum, existence, things like that.

I eventually wound up settling on Old Testament studies, mainly because of some inspiring teachers, two of dear and blessed memory, who led me to see that Christians who are serious about studying the Bible need to get a handle on all the begats, lists of animal sacrifices, laws, and those long, tedious, repetitive stories that don't know when to stop. As one professor told me, "Three-quarters of our own Bible is the Old Testament, so you need to learn what to do with it." Valid point. And it set my career path.

Owing to my obsession for controlling the universe through my brain, coupled with deep insecurities I only came to understand decades later, I was a straight "A" student. I applied to several Ph.D. programs and was admitted to the Near Eastern Languages and Civilizations program at Harvard University. To this day I'm still not sure how I got in. Maybe I was the fifth caller.

What I do know is that I was about to be challenged for the next few years far more than I could have understood at the time, and I would grow much more than I knew was possible. My journey was approaching . . .

Turning Point Number 2.

Concerning Camels' Backs and Beach Balls

I LEARNED A LOT IN SEMINARY and matured as a person and a Christian. But at a conservative Protestant school founded at the height of American fundamentalism in the early twentieth century (think Scopes monkey trial), a lot of things about the Bible—those parts that don't behave—were either nervously kept from the students or handled awkwardly.

The real suspects, our archenemies, were mainstream biblical scholars outside our conservative walls, sweepingly referred to as "liberals." We were often told they were "unfaithful" to the Bible, or "denied" what the Bible "plainly" said. Some professors cautioned us to mine only "safe" bits and pieces of what they said, and if we wandered too far down that liberal path, our confidence in the Bible would erode and we might wind up as atheists, warlocks, or worse—mainline Presbyterians.

But that kind of protective thinking only works if you stay within the castle walls. Biblical scholarship "out there" might not sit well with conservative thinking, but it's pretty darn persuasive to just about everyone else who studies the Bible.

At Harvard I experienced no Jason Bourne–like conspiracy to destroy Christianity, as some warned me. No one was tempting me to come over to the dark side and become a godless freethinking Ivy League tweed-and-turtleneck anarchist. My professors really didn't care what I believed. They just went about their business, modeling for me intellectual freedom and deep learning, and much of what they said made a whole lot of sense.

The more I read, listened, and thought, the more the Bible came together in new and compelling ways.

I never felt lied to by my seminary professors. They were good people and I will always have deep respect for them. But looking back, it seems we were all caught up in a system that exerted a deep, subliminal pressure on its members to conform—a system that apparently couldn't hold it together without exercising some serious information control.

It was getting harder to pretend that the old way would still work if I just gave it more time and applied some touch-up paint here and there. I was beginning to sense that the default conservatism of my seminary, and energetically defended by the ecclesiastical bodies that supported it, *needed* a well-behaved Bible, was bent on making sure it got one, didn't do a good job handling evidence to the contrary, and wasn't above shaming, shunning, or demonizing those who didn't play by the rules.

I was also beginning to mourn the fact that my life, filled with church, Christian college, and even seminary, produced a set of beliefs that could so quickly melt away simply by paying attention to a few lectures and reading some books over the course of a few months. I felt then, as I do more strongly now, that something was very wrong with that picture.

Still, shifting my thinking on the Bible did not mean I was losing my faith in God. In fact, I had the growing sense that God was inviting me down this path, encouraging it even. I was having my own uh-oh moments that would eventually lead to a transformation of my faith, not its death. I was in the very early stages of processing new information against the background of my familiar faith—which was both exciting and unnerving. Journeys tend to be that way.

A big transformative moment snuck up on me one afternoon—again, as most big moments do—when I was just sitting there minding my own business, unaware I was about to run into . . .

Turning Point Number 3.

In my second year of doctoral work, I made some money as a teaching assistant for a course of six hundred undergraduates called "The Bible and Its Interpreters." The professor was Jewish, the first Jewish professor who ever taught me the Bible. He wore a kippa, ate kosher, and read Hebrew as quickly and easily as I scan the sports page. Being taught by Jewish professors had a lasting and hugely positive impact on me (we'll come back to that later).

In this class, he would walk the students through some of the major stories of the Old Testament, starting with the creation story in Genesis, Adam and Eve, and so forth, and explain how Jewish interpreters of the Bible living a century or two before the time of Christ understood these stories.

I know that sounds obscure. I felt the same way at the time. Give it a minute.

On the fateful day in question, the topic was an odd episode in the story of Moses. The Israelites had just begun their famous forty-year sojourn through the desert after they had been liberated from Egyptian slavery. Water was a problem, seeing that they were in the desert and all. To solve the problem, at the *beginning* of the forty years at a place called Rephidim, Moses struck a rock with his staff and miraculously water poured out. Then, forty years later at the *end* of their wilderness period, in an *entirely different location* (Kadesh), Moses did it again.

This raises a question: Did they just get water *twice*, forty years apart? Surely they must have gotten water in between. I mean, they got the manna (bread from heaven) every day. So how did they get water in their forty-year desert journey between Rephidim and Kadesh? The Bible never tells us.

And here is where things get bizarre, and we are now full speed ahead to Turning Point Number 3.

Some creative, ancient Jewish interpreters came up with the perfectly insane idea that the rock at the beginning and the rock at the end were actually *one and the same rock.* "How can that be?" (asks any normal person). "Simple" (say these ancient Jewish interpreters of the Bible)· that one rock had "obviously" been *following the Israelites around in the desert for forty years,* sort of like a movable drinking fountain.

What, you don't see that? Ha, neither did I. I sat there shaking my head, wondering if parents knew this was costing them over $50,000 a year.

Then it happened.

The professor asked the class to turn to the New Testament, to a passage in one of the apostle Paul's letters. To be clear, we were now in *my* part of the Bible, the Jesus part.

In 1 Corinthians 10:4, the apostle Paul mentions—as if it's no big deal and everyone's on board—this *very same idea* of a rock following the Israelites around in the desert supplying water. He writes, "For they drank from the spiritual *rock that followed them,* and the rock was Christ." And not only was there a rock in the desert tagging along with Moses, but the rock, Paul says, was Jesus.

Uh-oh.

I had officially arrived at Turning Point Number 3. I felt like I was watching my whole view of the Bible collapse like a house of cards—there one minute, familiar and looking stable, and then gone the next minute with a good stiff wind.

Why was this moment so significant and unsettling for me? These early Jewish interpreters were interesting to read about, maybe even a little entertaining, like when they talked about a movable water-producing rock. But Paul?! No, not Paul!! He's a Christian. He's on *our side.* He is speaking for God and so he's not supposed to say stupid things like rocks follow people around in the desert to give them a drink.

I had met Paul for the first time, it seemed, and it struck me that this Paul probably wouldn't be allowed to teach biblical interpretation at the seminary that first introduced me to Paul.

This moment was the straw that broke the camel's back. All those beach balls I had managed to keep down below the surface now burst up through the water and shot into the air. Or, if you're not tired of my metaphors yet, I saw I could no longer keep the sheep in the pen. I had stepped over a threshold into the light (next to last metaphor) and was staring plainly right into the face of a Bible (final metaphor) that wasn't behaving itself and that I now *knew* I could no longer make behave.

The Bible seemed, well, exposed, stripped of its designer power suit and replaced with off-the-rack sweatpants from Marshalls. It wasn't as special anymore, a book kept by God at a safe distance from every other kind of book, acting according to the attractive trifold color brochure that church and seminary had handed me.

Call me a slow learner, but this Bible—including now the Jesus part—suddenly seemed disturbingly at home in its ancient world.

I left the huge lecture hall of Sanders Theater, spiritually and emotionally disoriented, and made my way to the bicycle rack—either to go home or ride into traffic, I can't remember which. I swung my knapsack over my shoulder and said—and this is an exact quote—"Toto, I don't think we're in Kansas anymore."

In a moment of crystal clarity, I knew I had a decision to make.

Door Number Three

THREE DOORS WERE STANDING BEFORE ME.

Door number one: I could *ignore* what I just heard that day in Sanders Theater, make believe that what just happened to me didn't happen, and go on with my life on spiritual and intellectual autopilot, keeping all those balls submerged somehow under water.

Door number two: I could take the door my tradition expected of me, which is to *push back against* what I just heard. I could become a "Bible defender," swimming against the stream to protect at all costs the demands of a faith that needs a well-behaved Bible. I could dedicate my life to "proving" somehow that, despite appearances, Paul would never actually buy in to such a silly idea about a rock that became a portable drinking fountain.

Door number three: I could *face* what I just saw, accept the challenge, and start thinking differently about the Bible. I could learn to ask ancient questions of the Bible rather than impose my own, trust God rather than myself, and embark on a long journey that would lead who knows where.

Doors one and two were not an option for me. In an instant, that ship had sailed and was long gone over the horizon. I knew I'd never be able to maintain my integrity if I walked through those doors. And I'd be staring at a lifetime of stress holding the Bible together and making it behave.

So that afternoon in the spring of 1991, I chose door number three, and, as in Robert Frost's famous poem, it's made all the difference. I can't say I didn't struggle, but I didn't lose my faith in God. Instead, looking back, I believe God helped push me through door number three. I still loved reading the Bible and was excited to keep learning—in fact, more so. But I knew my life had just taken a turn. I would let go of a well-behaved Bible and try to trust God without a safety net. I did not know where that would lead, but I knew there was no turning back.

The thought of taking this journey was, as I said, exciting and unsettling. And I was committed to it—emotionally, intellectually, and spiritually. But I eventually had to leave Harvard and return to the world of conservative church life and conservative Bible teaching. And not everyone in that world shared my experience. This is fine, of course. We don't all walk the same path.

On the other hand, practically speaking, some of those people included friends and family, along with ecclesiastical authorities—and those who signed my paychecks.

My commitment to follow through on my choice came with a cost. I tried very hard, for years, with complete transparency, to blend together old and new—the particular Christian tradition that birthed me and for which I had deep respect, and the bigger Bible I had come to know, was excited about, and could not deny without deceiving myself and others.

But my decision to go through door number three would eventually come to make me an outsider in my own community, a suspicious character, a rebel, one who could not be trusted to speak of God, lend money to, or watch your pets. I would in time lose a high-ranking tenured position at the very same seminary where my passion for the Bible was ignited as a student and where I had taught for fourteen years.

I became for a time, as many others have, the proverbial spiritual wanderer, a ship cut adrift from any shore, seeking a home, an identity. For a time I contemplated just scrapping the whole religion thing, at least the professional side of it, and becoming a barista and just playing bar-league softball. At least they have beer and give out trophies.

Choosing door number three cost me. But even during the darkest and most challenging times, I *never once regretted the choice to open door* number three and walk through.

I gradually came to see—as I continue to see more with the passing years—that moving on from my familiar patterns of life and thought was a gift from the good and wise God. I needed to learn (apparently the hard way) that trusting God is not the same thing as trusting the Bible—let alone my own ideas about the Bible. I believe God, in his mercy, taught me this.

Walking this path that leads out from door number three has helped me not only to rediscover the Bible, but—far more important—to experience God differently, more as a good and loving parent who enjoys letting his children figure things out than as a stern schoolteacher waiting to mark our lives full of red ink when we give wrong answers, a view that had been modeled to me, whether intentionally or unintentionally, for most of my Christian life.

I feel I have been given permission to be honest with myself and with God about a Bible that behaves so unBible-like without being told God is deeply disappointed in me for doing so and might turn on me any second.

I gained a Bible—and a God—I was free to converse with, complain to, talk back to, interrogate, and disagree with, not as an act of rebellion, but as an act of faith and trust, rather than needing to tiptoe around lest a grumpy God lash out with plague, famine, and sword if I get the Bible wrong—like an abusive, drunken father you don't want to wake from his nap.

I was learning to *trust* God enough (what a concept) to know that, like family (the Bible calls him "Father" after all), he will come through no matter what, that his love and commitment to me is deeper than how my brain happens to be processing information at any given moment, to trust that God will be with me, not despite the journey but precisely because I was trusting God enough to take it.

So What's My Point?

THE BIBLE ITSELF, taken on its own terms, raises difficult questions and challenges for faith. My goal for this book, then, is to assure people of faith that they do not need to feel anxious, disloyal, unfaithful, dirty, scared, or outcast for engaging these questions of the Bible, interrogating it, not liking some of it, exploring what it really says, and discerning like adult readers what we can learn from it on our own journey of faith.

I want you to know that you are not being disloyal to God or "rebelling" if you have trouble accepting, for example, that God would command his people to commit genocide.

I want you to know you are not alone. Hardly.

And perhaps some who have walked away from any faith in God, because the Bible just couldn't bear up under the impossible expectations placed on it, might take a second look and find a truer faith.

I want pious people to see that—judging by how the Bible actually behaves—God did not design scripture to be a hushed afternoon in an oak-paneled library. Instead, God has invited us to participate in a wrestling match, a forum for us to be stretched and to grow. Those are the kinds of disciples God desires. This book, in other words, is a giant permission slip to let the wrestling begin.

It helps to know we are not the first ones to accept that challenge. Christians have pored long and hard over scripture for centuries and, judging by the scads of denominations and churches in the world and across history, it's clear that a lot of wrestling with scripture is part of the Christian tradition and not everyone comes out at the same place.

Even more so, the history of Judaism is a lively tradition of wrestling openly with scripture and coming to diverse conclusions about how to handle it. More so than the Christian tradition, Judaism embraces debate as a vital *part* of its faith. Disagreements are *preserved* (not silenced or marginalized) in official core texts of Judaism, like the Talmud and medieval commentaries on the Bible. Opposing opinions sit side by side as monuments to this wrestling match with scripture—and with God.

As I mentioned, I was influenced at Harvard by Jewish professors as they introduced me to this rich history of struggling with the Bible. Though I still handle the Bible as a Christian, through their influence I also came to appreciate and embrace the spiritual benefit of keeping conversations open rather than closing them. That influence is written all over this book.

The Bible isn't a cookbook—deviate from the recipe and the soufflé falls flat. It's not an owner's manual—with detailed and complicated step-by-step instructions for using your brand-new all-in-one photocopier/FAX machine/scanner/DVR/home security system. It's not a legal contract—make sure you read the fine print and follow every word or get ready to be cast into the dungeon. It's not a manual of assembly—leave out a few bolts and the entire jungle gym collapses on your three-year-old.

When we open the Bible and read it, we are eavesdropping on an ancient spiritual journey. That journey was recorded over a thousand-year span of time, by different writers, with different personalities, at different times, under different circumstances, and for different reasons.

In the Bible, we read of encounters with God by ancient peoples, in *their* times and places, asking *their* questions, and expressed in language and ideas familiar to *them*. Those encounters with God were, I believe, genuine, authentic, and real. But they were also ancient—and that explains why the Bible behaves the way it does.

This kind of Bible—the Bible we have—just doesn't work well as a point-by-point exhaustive and timelessly binding list of instructions about God and the life of faith.

But it does work as *a model for our own spiritual journey*. An *inspired* model, in fact.

All of us on a journey of faith encounter God from our point of view. I don't mean God does our bidding or we control the engagement. I just mean that we are humans and not God (stop me if I'm going too fast here). As obvious as this seems, it's worth saying: we meet God as people defined by our moment in the human drama, products of who, where, and when we are. We ask *our* questions of God and encounter God in *our* time and place in language and ideas familiar to *us*, just like the ancient pilgrims of faith who gave us the Bible.

This is why the Bible is worth reading—not a sanitized and artificially well-behaved version that tells you what to do and think on every line, but the diverse, inconsistent, messy, sometimes bizarre one we have.

This Bible, which preserves ancient journeys of faith, models for us our own journeys. We recognize something of ourselves in the struggles, joys, triumphs, confusions, and despairs expressed by the biblical writers.

Rather than a rulebook—and we seriously have to switch metaphors here—the Bible is more a land we get to know by hiking through it and exploring its many paths and terrains. This land is both inviting and inspiring, but also unfamiliar, odd, and at points unsettling—even risky and precarious.

I believe God encourages us to explore this land—all of it—patiently, with discipline, in community, and above all with a sense that we, joining the long line of those who have gone before, will come to know ourselves better and God more deeply by accepting that challenge.

Ironically, a safe, well-behaved Bible gives us an easy side path to evade this journey of faith, to give the appearance of piety, and in doing so sells the Bible short. We respect the Bible most when we let it be what it is and learn from it rather than combing out the tangles to make it presentable. Only then are we prepared to respect our own journey, our own uneven and sometimes unsettling path of learning who this God is and what it means to connect with him.

We, like the ancient Israelites and the early followers of Jesus, encounter God not high up in the heavens, but in the here and now, through our own circumstances, our own ups and downs. That's how the Holy Bible, the Word of God, works as a book of spiritual comfort, guidance, and insight.

Three big controversial issues shaped my discovery that the Bible is not an instruction manual but instead a model for our spiritual journey:

1. God does a lot of killing and plaguing, orders others to do it (usually the Israelites), or stands by watching as the Israelites go ballistic on their own. Exhibit A is God's command that the Israelites exterminate the inhabitants of the land of Canaan so they could move in.
2. What the Bible says happened often didn't—at least not the way the Bible describes it. And sometimes different biblical authors have very different takes on what happened in the past.
3. The biblical writers often disagree, expressing diverse and contradictory points of view about God and what it means to be faithful to him.

These are big tipping points many faithful readers have when beholden to a circle-the-wagons approach to defending an owner's manual Bible. These aren't the only issues, but they hit the big challenges for modern readers of the Bible. And we will cover each in the chapters that follow.

We will also zero in on how the Gospel writers and the apostle Paul read their Bible. They clearly revered their Jewish heritage and their scripture (what Christians will later call the Old Testament), but they also saw that God was pushing them beyond it.

They believed that Jesus of Nazareth, Israel's Messiah, was God's *surprise* ending to Israel's story—a surprise because he was crucified and then raised from the dead. By anyone's standards at the time, messiahs weren't supposed to do that.

Jesus was God's climax to Israel's story, but he was not bound to that story. He pushed at its boundaries, transformed it, and at times left parts of it behind.

When we read the New Testament, we have a front row seat to watch the earliest Christian writers working through the implications of God's unexpected, reorienting move—a crucified and risen messiah. Christians today need to listen carefully to what these New Testament writers are telling us, that God is pushing us, too, beyond the printed page as we seek to commune with him through scripture.

So this book is about finding some space to be honest with ourselves about the Bible and trusting God in the process. Reading the Bible as God's Word means accepting its own invitation to walk alongside ancient pilgrims, grappling with the bumps and bruises, gaps and gashes, valleys and plains of their journeys, and in doing so see a reflection of our own.

When we choose that riskier path, we will not long remain as we are. We will change for the better. We will grow and find a deeper faith—and a deeper God—in the process. That is the invitation God puts before us with his holy book.

Accepting that invitation is what this book is about.

Chapter
Two

God Did *What*?!

How Not to Treat Other People

1514, THE WEST INDIES. Spanish settlers land near present-day Panama. Blessed by God and king, and armed with razor-sharp steel, they have to come to claim what is theirs—and they are not interested in negotiating. They have gold and land on their mind, and the current residents of "New Spain" are in the way. The Spanish governor and faithful servant of God, Pedro Arias Dávila, quickly gets down to business.

Over the next seven years, Dávila purges the land of its subhuman, godless residents. Dávila is gracious, however. All along his victory tour, he gives the unarmed natives a choice. They could either bow instantly to a king and a god they had never heard of, from a country they could not imagine, become slaves, and hand over all their gold; or they could be overrun by horses and be hacked to bits by swords, and whoever was left would be enslaved anyway and still lose their gold.

Spaniards had been "settling" the West Indies like this since 1493. The slaughter continued until 1552, when the Dominican friar Bartolomé de Las Casas wrote *A Short Account of the Destruction of the Indies,* a gruesome tell-all of the horrors he had witnessed over the years. He convinced the right people that exterminating a people in God's name because you want their land and their stuff probably wasn't on God's to-do list.

Christians today, like Las Casas, denounce genocide as evil. After all, it's hard to see Jesus, who gave his life for others, advocating the systematic extermination of a population. Plus, he told his followers that true children of God love and pray for their enemies.

Some of Israel's ancient prophets strummed a similar chord. The book of Isaiah says there will be a time when Israel's God will settle all disputes between nations without violent conflict. Swords and spears will be forged into farming tools; war and fear among nations will cease. All will be at peace, because the true God is a God of peace, not of war—and certainly not of an assembly-line slaughter of people from the wrong tribe.

Slight problem though. Earlier in the Old Testament, God also orders the Israelites to (ahem) enter the land of Canaan, march from town to town, and (embarrassing shuffle of feet) wipe out their pagan inhabitants—men, women, and children—and take over their fields and live in their houses.

To the Spaniards, the "Indians" were simply their contemporary version of Canaanites. The first Europeans to settle North America also tended to see it as their Promised Land and the local Native American population as Canaanites who had no divine right to the land, and their fate was similar. Evidence of this mentality is seen in the many East and Midwest towns given biblical names like (New) Canaan, Bethlehem, Jericho, and Bethel.

You don't have to be Stephen Hawking to figure this one out. Christians, taking the Bible as a how-to book, have killed pagans, taken their land, and rejoiced in God's goodness. I mean, if it's in the Bible, it can't be bad, right? RIGHT?

It's hard to appeal to the God of the Bible to condemn genocide today when the God of the Bible commanded genocide yesterday. This is what we call a theological problem. And it's a big one, not only because of the whole Canaanite business, but because violence seems to be God's preferred method of conflict resolution.

As early as the sixth chapter of the Bible, in the book of Genesis, God floods the entire earth and kills every living creature except Noah, his family, and the animals on the ark. Later God tests Abraham by commanding him to slit his son's throat as a sacrifice (though God stops Abraham at the last second once he knew Abraham would go through with it). In the Exodus story, God's tenth and final plague against the Egyptians is to strike down their firstborn, and then a few lines later he drowns the entire Egyptian army in the Red Sea.

Later in the book of Exodus three thousand Israelites who built an idolatrous "golden calf" are purged by their own people with God standing by. In the book of Leviticus, Aaron's priestly sons, Nadab and Abihu, are consumed by the fire of God for some unexplained misstep while officiating over the sacrifices. Numerous laws carry the death penalty, like worshipping other gods, blasphemy, working on the Sabbath (the prescribed day of rest), or adultery. And we're only in the third book of the Bible.

God killing people, both Israelites and others, isn't a last-ditch measure of an otherwise patient deity. It's the go-to punishment for disobedience. To put a fine point on it, this God is flat-out terrifying: he comes across as a perennially hacked-off warrior-god, more Megatron than heavenly Father.

We're not the first ones to be puzzled and bothered about God's violence in the Bible; both Christians and Jews have worked on this issue ever since there's been a Bible.

And hands down, God's command to slaughter the population of Canaan so the Israelites can take over the neighborhood strikes most readers as over the top. Atheist writers like Richard Dawkins in *The God Delusion* are only too happy to jump all over it to point out how the Christian "God of Love" handles conflict. How can Islam be condemned for promoting a warring God who smites the infidel (a common Christian summary of 9/11) when the Christian God in the Old Testament does pretty much the same thing, only without airplanes?

I take this portrait of God in the Bible seriously, but I don't accept it as the final word. Whatever we do, we certainly can't hide under a blanket and wish this away. Only in wrestling with this portion of scripture, in accepting its challenge, will we see how scripture itself is pointing us forward, to journey beyond these stories and see a much larger and far richer landscape beyond.

So let's talk about the Canaanites and why God gives the command to obliterate them from the face of the earth.

Those Wicked, Horrible Canaanites

GOD'S COMMAND to exterminate the Canaanites wasn't an afterthought. As the Israelites tell the story, the Canaanites were doomed from the start for something that happened nearly at the beginning of human history.

After the great flood, which killed every living creature not on the ark, and Noah and his family de-ark, Noah plants the first vineyard, makes wine, and gets drunk (maybe he needed to unwind). Like a college freshman, he collapses naked inside his tent in a drunken coma. His youngest son, Ham, enters the tent, sees him lying there, and goes out to tell his brothers, Shem and Japheth. Rather than gawking, the two brothers walk backward into the tent and cover their father with a garment.

It's hard to know exactly what's going on here, but, apparently, the two brothers handle the situation correctly whereas Ham doesn't. So, when Noah wakes up, he does what any normal father would do when faced with the same dilemma—he curses Ham's descendants forever.

Three guesses who Ham's descendants are (and the first two don't count): the Canaanites.

The very first words out of Noah's mouth aren't, "What a night! What *was* I thinking!? I'll never do that again!" Not even, "Ham! Get in here! Why did you look upon my nakedness?!" Instead he says, "Cursed be *Canaan;* lowest of slaves shall he be to *his brothers.*"

Mind you, Canaan is one of Ham's four sons, yet only he *and his entire bloodline* are doomed—which seems not only extreme but misdirected. Two of Ham's other sons are Cush and Mizraim, the ancestors of the Egyptians who held the Israelites in slavery, so how about cursing their bloodline?

What is it about *this* one son of Ham that dooms him and his descendants to a perpetual subhuman legacy of slavery to his brothers' descendants—which includes the Israelites, descendants of Shem (which is where we get "Semitic" from)?

It looks like whoever wrote this story has a bone to pick with the Canaanites.

If we read this in another ancient book, we'd call it propaganda—a story to justify, not explain, hatred of the Canaanites. At least that's what it looks like. Israel's later sworn enemies, the Canaanites, are set up as failures from the beginning, and no treatment—not even extermination—is too harsh for these people whose ancestor's father saw his father drunk and naked.

This isn't beginning well for the Canaanites, and it doesn't get any better.

The Canaanites make a second appearance a few pages later. Abraham, Israel's first ancestor and until recently a resident of Haran to the north, is guided by God on a tour of the land of Canaan—the land he is promising to give to Abraham's descendants hundreds of years hence.

Tucked away in this story is what might look like a throwaway line by the narrator of the story, only it's not: "*At that time,* the Canaanites were in the land." In other words, "for now, but one day won't be." A small reminder of what is in store for the original occupants of Canaan.

Further on, still in the book of Genesis, God repeats the promise to give the land of the Canaanites (here called "Amorites") to Abraham's descendants. But before that happens, we learn that at some future time the Israelites would first be slaves in a foreign country (Egypt) for four generations before they take the land. In the meantime, God will allow the Canaanites to remain where they are.

Why the delay? To give the Canaanites enough rope with which to hang themselves—with each passing generation they will grow more and more wicked. That way, when the day of reckoning comes (and it assuredly will), the Canaanites will be all the more deserving of everything they get.

No heads-up. No chance to turn things around. For some reason, among all the nations of the earth, the Canaanites will be left to grow like ugly weeds to be mowed down when they are good and ripe.

Hundreds of years later, just as God had said to Abraham, the Israelites find themselves in Egypt as slaves, living in a ghetto, building cities for Pharaoh. Through Moses they are rescued and make their way to Mount Sinai. There they receive instructions from God (the Law of Moses, a.k.a. Torah) about conduct toward one another and how to worship God the right way. With that under their belts, it's time to pack up and leave for their new home promised to Abraham long ago.

For the Canaanites—the ancient enemy, doomed from the start, and current residents of the land—things were about to get ugly.

As a preview of what is to come, along the way from Mount Sinai to claim their land, whenever they broke camp and set out on their journey, the Israelites would sing a rousing battle song: *Rise up, O Lord! May your enemies be scattered; may your foes flee before you.*

Those living in towns along Israel's path—tending their flocks, growing their grain, feeding their children, basically minding their own business—are *God's* enemies, which hardly seems, shall I say, fair. What did they do to become a pregame warm-up for the invasion of Canaan?

To sum up: so far, God's plan to form a nation out of Abraham's descendants is punctuated by a foreboding sense that the Canaanites are dead meat.

Marching Orders

THE ISRAELITES reach the border of Canaan, and Moses sends out spies to scope out the land. How many people are there? Are they strong or weak? Are their towns walled or fortified? What is the soil like? Are there trees? Translation: What's our new home like, and how efficiently can we expect to kill the Canaanites and minimize our own losses?

The spies report to Moses that the land is beautiful, "flowing with milk and honey," a paradise-like plot of land, brimming with herds ("milk") and produce ("honey," i.e., nectar)—the jackpot, by ancient standards. But the Canaanites look like a rough crowd. They are powerful and numerous and live in huge fortified cities. Even giants live among them, offspring of the ancient union between gods and human women we read about just before the story of Noah's flood.

The spies panic and spread a rumor that the land is actually pretty dumpy, and with giants and all, it's best just to keep moving, and God will understand. Only he doesn't. Israel's lack of nerve so angers God that he puts the conquest of Canaan on hold for forty years so the Israelites could wander in the wilderness, ample time to let that faithless generation die out and knock some sense into the others.

Fast-forward forty years—let's try it again.

The punishment period is over, and the Israelites are once again poised to invade Canaan. To make sure they get it right this time, God outlines specific marching orders—and if you're not convinced by now that the Canaanites are done for, maybe this will help.

> Don't be afraid (like forty years ago), because I will be with you. And here's what you're going to do.
>
> *On the way to Canaan,* whenever you come across a city that is outside of its borders, first offer terms of peace. If they accept, enslave the people. If they refuse, kill the men. You can keep the women, children, livestock, and anything else for yourself as spoils of war.
>
> *But when you enter Canaan,* the land I am giving you, as I promised to Abraham long ago, do not offer terms of peace, but kill everything that breathes—including women, children, and livestock. Leave nothing alive. Otherwise you may be tempted to worship other gods.

No need to be afraid to attack and kill, because God will be right there with them making sure they come up winners. He will be at the side of the Israelite soldiers as they gut young non-Canaanite husbands and take their wives and children into slavery. He will stand watch as they run their swords through every living thing in Canaan: men, boys, infants, someone's grandmother, or pregnant wife, and even livestock. God will be with the Israelites, pleased as they level town after town, deaf to screams and cries for mercy.

This takes my breath away. It's enough to make you want to stop reading.

The marching orders are carried out by Joshua, Moses's successor and all-around fierce fighting guy.

The first cities to go are Jericho and Ai. Next, kings from the coastal area get together to fight back. Among them are the Gibeonites, who trick Joshua into making a treaty with them ("Uh . . . why, no, we're not from around here. No need to wipe us out. How about a peace treaty?"). When the ruse is found out, Joshua is honor-bound to his oath, so he enslaves them instead to become "hewers of wood and drawers of water" for the people of God.

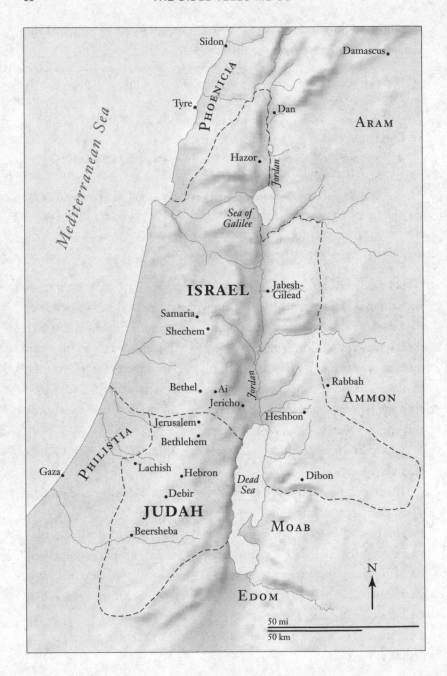

Shame. Had Joshua not been asleep at the switch, the Israelites could have killed the Gibeonites, too.

Next up are the kings of five towns who are cowering in a cave. Joshua orders that the cave be blocked with rocks to prevent their escape while his army chases after their armies, which leaves only a few survivors (God be praised). Satisfied with a good day's work, Joshua returns to the cave, brings out the five kings, has their heads cut off, and hangs their bodies on trees until evening—and I'm having as much trouble processing that as you are. To encourage his troops, Joshua tells them not to be afraid, for God will do this to all their enemies.

The book of Joshua lists thirty-one Canaanite towns now under Israelite control with still more lands remaining to be conquered. (Other towns on the other side of the Jordan River were also conquered, which we read about elsewhere.) The book ends with the twelve tribes of Israel carving the land up between them and renewing their commitment to the God who brought them out of Egypt and who kindly gave them this land to live in, and generally sitting back and admiring a job well done.

The action continues in the next book of the Bible, Judges. But here we read, surprisingly, that the Israelites under Joshua actually didn't purge the land completely. Some Canaanites are left hanging around, while others are made slaves—not at all what God had ordered. Sure enough, just as God feared, these Canaanites lead the Israelites astray with their false gods, which angers God because he did not bring Israelites to Canaan to share them with the likes of the storm god Baal or the fertility goddess Asherah.

But rather than giving them another talking to about how the Canaanites needed to be wiped out, God leaves the Canaanites right where they are to test whether the Israelites would really remain faithful to him. They will also serve a darker purpose in God's plan: a whole new generation of Israelites that hadn't experienced the glories of war will practice waging war on live Canaanite tackling dummies.

And practice makes perfect. Canaanites would gradually fade from the scene, although the Canaanite influence of worshipping the wrong gods remains a constant problem throughout Israel's period of the monarchy leading to their exile to Babylon.

Bottom line, the extermination of the Canaanites is not an afterthought. According to the Bible, Israel's God planned it from the days of Noah and the flood, and he carries out the plan with bracing determination and precision, patiently encouraging and even training the troops to get it done.

"If Jesus Sends People to Hell, What's So Bad About Killing Some Canaanites??"

MANY BIBLE READERS FEEL the strong impulse to get God off the hook for acting this way, which means finding a good way to end the following sentence: "It's a perfectly fine and right thing for God to order the extermination of Canaanites and take their land because . . ."

The need to end that sentence well comes from an owner's manual mentality about the Bible: What the Bible tells us about God simply *has* to be the way God is. God said it; I must believe it; and so it must be true. That mentality has produced all sorts of stressful solutions, not to mention a few atrocities.

Here is one example some Christians resort to (which you have probably heard before): *God is the sovereign king of the universe, and his unfathomable will is not to be questioned by puny mortals, so shut up about it.*

That's simple and straightforward, I'll give you that. But after the dust settles and we are left with our thoughts, we might ask ourselves, *Is this really the kind of God we believe in, the God who created the world and loves it? Is this the God that greets us when we rise in the morning and think of when the day closes? Is this the kind of God we tell others about, or do we opt for the nicer version, since we know the other version won't cut it?* Westboro Baptist Church might get giddy over a God like this, but they're wacky. I wouldn't trust them to save a drowning kitten.

This really isn't a solution, anyway. It's simply restating the problem: God orders his subjects to kill Canaanites. The question remains, "Why is God acting like Zeus or a fascist dictator?"

Here is another strategy for the sentence completion exercise: *Sure, Jesus talks about loving your enemies, but Jesus also talks about throwing sinners into hell to burn forever.* Since eternal damnation is far worse than exterminating merely one ancient people for their land, the argument goes, don't get all worked up about the Canaanites. Crisis averted.

No, it's not.

Just so we don't get off on the wrong foot, let's all agree that Jesus wasn't a meek and mild peacenik. He, along with the Old Testament and his fellow Jews, believed that "wrath" was a perfectly good word to describe how God feels about sin. But that's got nothing to do with *hell*—at least what Jesus means by it.

For one thing, our idea of "hell," with demons, pitchforks, and eternal flaming agony, comes to us by way of medieval Christian theology. That idea of hell isn't found in the Bible.

Actually, we'd be best off just dropping using the word "hell" altogether, since even Jesus never uses it. In the Gospels the word is *Gehenna,* which is a Greek translation of the Old Testament Hebrew *ge' hinnom* meaning "Valley of Hinnom"—an actual valley located just outside the walls of Jerusalem. The Old Testament prophet Jeremiah has issues with the Valley of Hinnom: the residents of Jerusalem sacrificed their children there to foreign gods.

Now, if you know your Old Testament, there are few worse things that Israelites can do than roast their kids to foreign gods. So Jeremiah warns the people of Jerusalem that God will soon punish them by sending the dreaded Babylonians to destroy Jerusalem (which happened in 586 BCE).

These invaders would slaughter so many Jerusalemites, according to Jeremiah, that this "Valley of Hinnom" would overflow with *their* corpses for the birds and wild animals to munch on.

Tit for tat: the valley where they sacrificed their children with fire would become the place of their own punishment—"going to hell," so to speak.

The book of Isaiah picks up on this idea and adds an unquenchable fire that will burn the bodies of the slain that rebelled against God. Obviously the author of Isaiah is not talking about a place under the ground where bad people go to burn forever after they die (although Christians often read it that way).

"Valley of Hinnom," later *Gehenna,* refers to God's punishment to come upon his own people for failing to recognize God's presence and follow God's ways. Jesus, preaching to his fellow Jews, jumped all over this symbolism of God's punishment.

Soon (in 70 CE, to be exact) the Romans would come and level Jerusalem, as the Babylonians had done before, leaving the streets running red with blood. As in the days of Jeremiah, God will once again bring judgment on the residents of Jerusalem, though this time not for roasting children, but for failing to accept Jesus as God's messiah for the kingdom of God that was, right now, in their midst.

"Hell" is a tricky subject, and a lot more could be said, but let's stick with the point. What Jesus means by "hell" isn't worse than what God did to the Canaanites. "Hell" doesn't get God off the hook because it's off topic.

If you want to know what Jesus thinks about Canaanites, just ask him—though you have to pay attention to see it.

The Gospels of Matthew and Mark contain a story of a woman who begs Jesus to heal her daughter. In Mark's Gospel, the woman is from "Syrian Phoenicia," a region to the north *outside* of Judea (what Israel was called at that time). But, in Matthew's Gospel she is a Canaanite woman, which is the only time Israel's ancient foes are mentioned in the New Testament.

This sounds like something we should pay attention to.

At first Jesus plays it cool and ignores the Canaanite woman's cries for help. Then he tells her he only has time to help his own people. He even calls this Canaanite woman a dog waiting for crumbs at the master's table, but she keeps at it. Finally Jesus, shockingly, rewards her for her great faith.

The only time a Canaanite makes it into the New Testament, and she becomes a model of faithful persistence: her faith in Jesus led to her daughter's healing.

This woman isn't really a Canaanite. Matthew just calls her that—like he had a point to make about what God thinks of outsiders and how followers of Jesus are to think of them, too.

If there were any "Canaanites" in Jesus's day—Gentiles living in the Holy Land—it was the Romans. Tensions often ran high among various Jewish groups about how to relate to their Gentile overlords. Jewish responses varied. Some seemed poised to fight and rid the land of them. Others took a "live and let live" approach. Others sidled up to the Romans for their own political advantage. I'm sure there were other points of view circulating among the everyday people that haven't been preserved for us through the centuries.

Here is Jesus's response.

My kingdom is not of this world.
Love your enemies, pray for those who persecute you, that you may
         be sons of your father in heaven.
Blessed are the meek, for they will inherit the earth.
Blessed are the peacemakers, for they will be called sons of God.

Jesus had no interest in spreading hatred, and certainly not in starting a holy war—replacing one violent regime with another. According to Jesus, who claimed to speak for God, God was done with that sort of thing.

To sum up: if you want to try and get God off the hook for exterminating Canaanites, leave Jesus out of it. Nothing Jesus said or did is worse than God telling Israelites to kill Canaanite families, take their land, live in their houses, and grow crops in their fields. Jesus was against it.

Here is another attempt at justifying God's action against the Canaanites: *Waging war in order to survive was inevitable during that time.* That's true. In the world of the ancient Israelites, waging war to preserve your land and take other people's land from them was like heading over to 7-Eleven for the daily paper.

But does this mean that God's hands were tied, that he had to buy into the system? He's God, right? Was there really *no* other way?

And why would he be so intent on making Israel a nation in the first place, thus putting its people in a position of *having* to defend their borders or expand them by killing—not to mention plundering and pillaging?

Plus, the Israelites weren't defending their borders against the Canaanites. They were the aggressors.

Why didn't God just find some other way so that the Israelites could live among the Canaanites to influence them peacefully? Instead of equipping the Israelites to kill Canaanites, why not equip them to block out the temptation to worship other gods?

Why? Because, the biblical writers believed, God is a warrior who likes waging war against the enemy and acquiring land. He doesn't buy into the system reluctantly. War brings him honor and glory.

But again, Jesus, taking a page from some of the Old Testament prophets (like Isaiah), would complicate things. God's people are a light that shines into dark places, or salt that makes the whole meal taste good, or a pinch of yeast that makes the entire loaf rise. Wherever God's people are, it makes a difference—for the better, and without violence.

So here is the question people have been asking for a very long time: Why didn't God just enact that policy earlier? Why wait? Have the Canaanites over for dinner. Invite them to church. Send over a fruit basket. Something. Anything. Maybe the Canaanites would have preferred that option—or at least it couldn't have hurt to ask.

God's Nicer Side

SOME TRY to get God off the hook by claiming, *Sure, God killed Canaan-*
ites, but we have to balance it out with those parts where God was nicer.

Does a nicer side of God really "balance" anything? What kind of God
goes off balance in the first place? When a fifth-grade bully takes a break
for a few days from extorting milk money from the third graders, his bul-
lying isn't "balanced." ("See, kids, he's not *always* mean. Just remember
that next time he shakes you down.")

It's certainly true, though, that the Old Testament portrays various
sides of God in diverse ways, and we shouldn't forget it (and I won't let you,
because we will come back to this in chapter 4). After all, the Old Testament is a library of books, written at different times, for different reasons,
and from different perspectives. And yes, God is not always looking to
shed blood. He is also called gracious, compassionate, slow to anger, rich
in love, and good to all. He says he doesn't want the wicked to perish but
turn from their wicked ways.

This sounds promising. Maybe mass killing of Canaanites is an exception to the rule and compassion is the real side of God.

Not quite. God almost always says these kind and gracious things *to*
the Israelites. And that's the whole problem: he is *their* God; he has never-
ending compassion on *them* (with an occasional mass slaying or plaguing). This doesn't take the edge off what he does to the Canaanites (or

other nations that get in the way). In fact, exterminating the Canaanites and giving their land to them *was* a way that God showed kindness to the Israelites.

Still, with all that, we definitely find moments where Israel's God has compassion for the nations of the world. A key moment is the book of Jonah. God had told Jonah to preach a message of repentance to the people of Nineveh, the capital of one of Israel's constant nemeses and all-around horrible nation to get on the wrong side of: Assyria.

Assyrians had no problem impaling or flaying their captives. They also conquered and deported most of the ancient Israelites (722 BCE), the northern half, never to be heard from again. God telling Jonah to "preach repentance" to the Assyrians rather than sending an army to wipe them out was out of character—having mercy on the enemy.

Jonah doesn't like God's change of heart, and he lets him know it. What if the Ninevites actually repent and God winds up having compassion for them? What a disaster. So he hops a slow boat headed in the opposite direction, which eventually earns him an all-expenses-paid weekend stay in the belly of a big fish.

Eventually, dragging his feet all the way, Jonah makes it to Nineveh to deliver God's message. And just as he feared, it works: the Ninevites have repentance coming out of their ears, which annoys Jonah and drives him to a pity party. God cares about Israel's enemies.

On the other hand, two books to the right, we find the book of Nahum, another prophet. Here it's business as usual concerning the Assyrians: God will wipe them out and show them no mercy. The book of Nahum ends with God gloating over the destruction of hated Nineveh and a global high five over Nineveh's fatal undoing.

In my opinion, the book of Jonah gives us a look at the Israelites thinking out loud about this "us versus them" mentality that we see most everywhere else in the Old Testament. Jonah versus Nahum is a good example of the kind of diverse thinking we find in the Bible, which, as I said, we'll hit in chapter 4. But, for here, we just need to see that the tension between "Assyrians all need to die" to "maybe God cares for them, too" *doesn't balance the Canaanite situation*. It's an exception to the rule.

Plus, for true balance, you'd need a prophet like Jonah to preach repentance to *Canaanites*. But that never happens.

The only example of mercy toward Canaanites—to be precise, *one* Canaanite—is in the story of Jericho, the first Canaanite city to fall under Joshua's command. Two Israelite spies scope out the city and pay a visit to the prostitute Rahab. Rather than turning them in, she hides them and makes them promise to spare her and her family. She has heard all about Israel's God and knows a winner when she sees one.

Rahab the Canaanite prostitute and her family are spared, but this is a onetime deal and doesn't "balance" God's marching orders, as if God had a change of heart or never really meant it. Those orders didn't mention what to do if a Canaanite *defects*, but now that it happened, they all go with the flow and she and her family are spared.

Actually, the whole reason Rahab defects is because she is scared out of her wits: the bloody reputation of Israel's warrior-God was becoming world news. And clearly, judging by the wars that follow, there is no letup toward the Canaanites on God's part.

Like the Jonah story, the story of the Canaanite prostitute Rahab may give us a glimpse of the Israelites' thinking about what it means to be an "insider" or an "outsider" to God. Is God really interested solely in being the God of one people, or is there room for non-Israelites to share in God's kindness (the same point Jesus and Paul would eventually make)? The Rahab story might even suggest that the writer has an issue with "us versus them" thinking elsewhere in the Bible, but that's hard to know and more than we need to get into here.

Bottom line, these examples of God's kindness to non-Israelites are valuable and shouldn't be dismissed. In fact, they already encourage us to see how the ancient Israelites saw God as more than a tribal deity. My only point is that these stories don't erase God's command to exterminate the Canaanites. The fact remains they were singled out for massacre because they occupied land God intended to give to the Israelites.

Israel can, in principle, coexist with other nations—as long as everyone behaves and keeps their distance. But you can't have God's people sharing living space and intermingling with unclean pagans.

That's why the Canaanites are exterminated. There is no way to balance that.

Worst. Sinners. Ever.

ANOTHER APPROACH to getting God off the hook is to say, *The Canaanites got exactly what they deserved because they were utterly morally corrupt.* This explanation has something going for it, at least on the surface. In a few places, God tells the Israelites that the Canaanites must die because of their gross immorality, like bestiality and incest, not to mention sacrificing their children to their gods.

As the argument goes, exterminating these horrific pagan sinners doesn't make God a moral monster at all! God is simply playing his role of just judge of the world, showing his holy and uncompromising intolerance of sin and punishing sinners as they deserve. It's actually *more* remarkable that he doesn't do this all the time.

Some defenders of this view go so far as to say that wiping out the Canaanites is a sneak preview of the end of the world and a warning to us all. The Canaanites are getting *now* what all sinners will get later on in the final judgment when God will kill a lot more people (a view found in a literal reading of the last book of the Christian Bible, the book of Revelation).

This solution is common among some Christians. But once you start picking at it, it comes apart pretty quickly.

For one thing, giving Canaanites first prize in the "worst sinners ever" contest is a caricature, and a bit of propaganda. Were they really *so* bad that they and they *alone* deserved to be annihilated—old to young, male and female, even animals?

Take one of the Canaanites' gross sins, child sacrifice. The Canaanites hadn't cornered the market on the idea. Child sacrifice was common.

An example comes from the Bible. King Mesha of Moab, right across the Jordan River, is losing a battle against a coalition of forces led by Israelites. Backed into his own end zone, he calls an audible and throws a desperation pass the length of the field—he sacrifices his own son on the city walls to appease his god Kemosh in order to gain victory. (It worked, by the way. The forces had to withdraw and Mesha was saved.) So other people back then sacrificed children, not just Canaanites, and they weren't wiped off the face of the earth.

We even have some rather disturbing examples from the Bible where child sacrifice seems to be something God is perfectly fine with. God himself tells Abraham to kill his son Isaac as a sacrifice. At the last second God puts a stop to it, but that doesn't mean he wasn't serious. God was testing Abraham, as the story tells us, to see how obedient he was—and it wouldn't have been a real test if there wasn't a real chance that Abraham could have gone through with it.

Then we have Jephthah, one of Israel's last judges, who pledges to sacrifice to God whatever walked out of the door of his house if God gave him victory in battle. Sure enough, out comes his daughter (was he expecting a cow or something?) and after a mourning period God gets his sacrifice.

Eventually we must confront the truth. However immoral the Canaanites were, the real problem isn't *what* they did, but *where* they did it.

They were contaminating the land that God set aside for the Israelites since the days of Abraham and so had to be exterminated. Take any other people group and put them in the land of Canaan, and *they* would be the ones tasting Israelite steel, and *their* immorality would be described as the worst ever. Take the Canaanites and put them somewhere else, and we'd never hear about them.

The Canaanites' main sin was their street address. That is why *they* had to be eliminated.

And what about the command to kill the Canaanite children?

Some justify this by saying that the children were somehow infected by their parents' wickedness, so God was good and just to kill them, too. They deserved it. But the Bible never offers that explanation, even remotely, and the only reason to make it up is a desperate attempt to get God off the hook.

Of course, as we all know, little Canaanite boys grow up to be big Canaanite soldiers, so, as some argue, perhaps it's best to off them right here and now and avoid endless warfare. Awkward moment: in the first chapter of the book of Exodus, Pharaoh gives the same reason for throwing male Israelite babies into the Nile to drown. So God's MO mirrors that of the Egyptians.

Another problem with the "Canaanites deserved it" idea is that God's treatment of non-Canaanites isn't much better—and this is a huge problem.

According to the original marching orders God gave the Israelites that we saw earlier, residents of non-Canaanite towns became slaves if they surrender. If not, only the men are to be killed. The woman and children still become slaves.

Hold that thought.

Earlier in the Bible (book of Numbers), the Israelites are told by God to wage war against the Midianites for their role (this gets confusing) in leading the Israelite men to have sex with Moabite women and worshipping the false god Baal a few chapters earlier.

Long story short, the Israelites win. They kill all the men and all the women who had seduced the Israelite men. They also kill *all the boys* (wouldn't want them to grow up to breed and be soldiers). That is horrific enough, but they also divide up the virgin women/girls among the soldiers and the rest of the community as spoils of war.

And God doesn't step in and put a stop to it.

Anyone who thinks that God's extermination of Canaanites is good and just has to argue the same way for God's treatment of virgin women and children as spoils of war. I don't think we want to go there.

To sum up: Why did God single out the Canaanites for extermination? The factor that distinguished the Canaanites from everyone else, the reason they "deserved" to be exterminated, wasn't their immorality, but the fact that they (like everyone else) were an immoral people who *occupied the land* God promised to give the Israelites. To leave any Canaanites alive would (1) contaminate the land and (2) threaten Israel's devotion to their God.

*   *   *

It is what it is and there is no getting around it. If we were reading a story like this in some other religious text, we'd call this genocide, ethnic cleansing, and barbarous—pure and simple.

I've held off drawing this analogy, but to call for the extermination of a group of people (defined by their culture and religion), to grab their land and stuff, and to justify it by saying God told you to do it because those people are impure, dirty, worthy only of death—well, we've seen this up close in recent history.

In the past one hundred years, the estimates of the number of dead from just six of the best-known ideologically driven genocides—Armenia, the Holocaust, Soviet famine, Cambodia, Rwanda, and Darfur—range from about 10.7 million (Yankee Stadium filled to the brim and swept clean two hundred times) to 27.4 million (the population of New York and New Jersey combined). Most know this sort of thing is wrong—even if it's in the Bible.

A lot of deeply unsatisfying answers are out there. I think they are wrongheaded and cause more stress to defend than they are worth. Now the question is how to move forward.

Is there a better way to think about Canaanite extermination that doesn't get God cheaply off the hook but that also doesn't make him look like a Balrog? (Non-Tolkien fans please Google.)

Yes there is. But you might want to get a snack or something, maybe rehydrate. We can't rush this next part.

It's a Tribal Culture Thing

TO MOVE FORWARD, we need to look at the Canaanite issue from a different, and perhaps very new, angle. And here it is: God never told the Israelites to kill the Canaanites. The Israelites believed that God told them to kill the Canaanites.

This may not sound like a promising start—and some of you may need a moment to walk across the room and pick this book up—but give it a chance. I'm not ignoring a part of the Bible that I just happen to find offensive. I'm not arbitrarily picking and choosing what to keep and what to throw out. Really.

I am respecting the Bible's *ancient voice,* trying to understand what that ancient voice is saying, and *then* (and only then) make a decision, as best as I can, about what to do with it. Where the "get God off the hook" solutions all falter is that they are not asking ancient questions, but modern ones.

Listening to the ancient voice of the Bible means asking *why* Canaanite extermination is in the Old Testament at all and how it would have been heard at that time.

To answer these questions, we need to step outside of the Bible and into the world of the Bible. Doing so will help us see that respecting the Bible does not require us to endorse everything the Bible says about God or Israel's past. The Bible won't fall apart in the process. Neither will God. Neither should we.

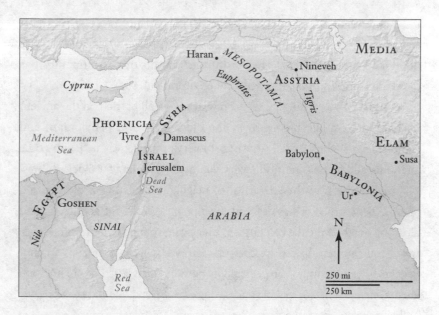

The Israelites are God's Chosen People, but they didn't drop out of the sky. The Israelites grew up out of the soil of an ancient world, from a small band of tribes and nomads to become a nation, one surrounded by older and larger superpowers: Babylon to the east, Assyria to the north, and Egypt to the south.

These nations were already a millennium or two old with ancient customs and stories of their own by the time baby Israel came on the scene and began settling its land (judging by the biblical and archaeological evidence, probably somewhere in the thirteenth century BCE—more later).

The older cultures of Israel's superpower neighbors, not to mention the older native Canaanite culture within which Israel emerged, helped shape Israelite culture. By "shaped" I don't mean Israel's culture was merely a cheap imitation of other cultures. Israel was its own nation with its own distinctive beliefs and practices.

Still, so much of Israel's culture looks very similar to what we see elsewhere in the ancient world. Israel's system of laws, worship practices, notions of kingship, style of poetry, attitudes toward women and slaves, ideas about how the cosmos was created, and on and on, were unquestionably shaped by its time and place—which is to say, Israel's culture developed the way every other culture in the history of humanity has developed: as part of a larger cultural environment.

Even Israel's own language, Hebrew, was a small branch on the ancient language tree, a late bloom from the older Assyrian, Babylonian, and Canaanite branches. Israel, in almost every respect, was a "Jacob come lately," a child of the time, and a very young child among far older siblings.

The Israelites also shared with their neighbors a tribal view of the world around them, which brings us to our next point: "We are the good guys, and all of you out there are the bad guys. We hate you, your gods, and your strange ways. You threaten us and we distrust you. We will make treaties when it benefits us, and we may even get friendly now and then. But, bottom line, you are the enemy. When we get big and strong enough, and our god favors us, we will invade you. You are not 'us.' You are 'them.' Watch your back."

Taking land and defeating enemies with the blessing of the gods was as common in the ancient world as Dunkin' Donuts in New England. And, as the Canaanite extermination story shows, the Israelites were every bit as much a part of that mentality as any other ancient culture we can point to.

A ninth century BCE stone monument from Moab, one of Israel's next-door neighbors to the east mentioned earlier (see map on page 38), illustrates how the Canaanite extermination in the Old Testament fits in an ancient mind-set. On this monument is carved a revealing—if also boastful and exaggerated—record of the Moabite king Mesha's military campaign against the Israelites.

The Israelites had been in control of Moab for some time, and the reason, Mesha tells us, has *nothing* to do with Israel's might (of course not, why would you think that?), but because his god Kemosh was angry with Moab (yeah, that's it). Allowing foreigners to overrun them was Kemosh's punishment. Even when Moab is down, Moab's god is still in control.

But now all is right again between Kemosh and Moab, and Mesha is given the thumbs-up to go through the towns of Moab and *kill all the Isra-elites as a sacrifice to Kemosh and take back the land that rightfully belongs to them*. When Mesha got to the town of Nebo, we read that he "put to the ban" the entire town, meaning he killed *the entire population,* seven thousand people in all, as an act of devotion to Kemosh.

If you think this sounds like what we read in the Bible, join the club. Both Mesha and Moses (and later Joshua) were told by their deity to invade a land they believed rightfully belonged to them and "put to the ban" the entire population as an act of devotion and obedience to God. Hebrew and Moabite are very similar languages, and they even use the same word for this ban. (Impress your friends, rivals, and that cute new neighbor in 3B: the word is *cherem,* pronounced with a throaty "ch" as in "Bach.")

Failure to "put to the ban" everyone and everything as directed by your god was a great way to make your god extremely angry—including Israel's God. Right after the conquest of Jericho, God turns his back on Israel's next battle against the town of Ai (pronounced "eye," not "A-eye"; if you hear anyone pronouncing it A-eye, you may put them to the ban). The Israelites are routed, and they soon learned why God had withdrawn his hand.

A guy named Achan did not honor the "ban" against Ai, meaning he kept some of the stuff for himself. This angered God, and Israel's victory tour through Canaan would only continue by appeasing that anger. That meant executing Achan and his whole family. Tit for tat: Achan was subjected to the same ban that he violated.

Israel was an ancient tribal people, and they thought and acted like one. But knowing that doesn't really solve our problem, does it? It just makes us think that Israel's God had the same hang-ups as all the other gods, just with another name. Instead of buying into the system, why didn't he just take all this barbaric tribal nonsense in another direction?

Before we get to that, we first need to throw another factor into the mix, and it can be a tough hill to climb.

I told you to rehydrate.

Digging for Answers

BIBLICAL ARCHAEOLOGISTS are about as certain as you can be about these things that the conquest of Canaan as the Bible describes did not happen: no mass invasion from the outside by an Israelite army, and no extermination of Canaanites as God commanded.

This bit of information may feel like pipes bursting down into your living room, but stay with it. It may wind up being a bit of unexpected good news.

First off, I don't worship at the altar of what archaeologists say, and neither should you. "Some of my best friends are archaeologists," but, like a lot of academics, they're not always right, they disagree with each other, they can have blind spots like the rest of us mortals, and sensationalized "discoveries" flood the Internet ("We found the fork Moses used at the first Passover!"). Some archaeologists even get pretty Rambo on you to protect their theories, which only adds to the hype. Plus, a lot about Israel's past is murky or simply shrouded in mystery and probably unrecoverable through archaeology.

That being said, archaeologists aren't kids playing in a sandbox, and they're certainly not idiots. They may not be able to uncover all of Israel's past, but they are trained and experienced scholars, and the better ones know their limitations.

One thing archaeologists can tell us is whether or not a city was violently destroyed by outside invaders, and whether a new people group took up residence. Battles and destructions of cities leave archaeological footprints—things like soot (if the town was burned), weapons, smashed pottery, and human bones. Mass migrations of people groups, as the Bible describes with Israel entering Canaan, would cause some cultural upheaval and leave some sort of remains for archaeologists to dig up and write long books about to help them get tenure.

Remember those thirty-one Canaanite towns listed in the book of Joshua (plus four other towns on the other side of the Jordan River)? Sixteen towns were destroyed according to the stories in the books of Numbers, Joshua, and Judges. Of those sixteen, two or three, maybe four, cities show signs of violent destruction at or around the time when Joshua and his army would have been plowing through Canaan (thirteenth century BCE, about two hundred years before the time of King David). That's it.

The towns on the other side of the Jordan River, in Moab, don't look like they were even occupied at the time.

We also read in the Bible that twelve towns were taken over without a fight. But of those twelve, only seven were even occupied at the time, according to archaeological findings. And of those same twelve towns that the Bible says weren't destroyed, three actually *do* show signs of destruction.

In other words, archaeology and the biblical story don't line up well at all.

Jericho, the first of the towns to be razed in the book of Joshua, is the most famous example. Not only was Jericho minimally inhabited at best at the time, but it had no massive protective walls, which means the biblical story of the "walls of Jericho" tumbling down is a problem—at least that's what a hundred years of digging there has shown us.

The two cities that fit best with what we read in Joshua are Bethel and Hazor, and perhaps a third, Debir. Another city, Lachish was also destroyed, but probably about one hundred years later—long after the swift victory tour described in the book of Joshua (see map on page 38).

Archaeologically speaking, there is no sure way of knowing who was responsible, but nothing says, "outsiders were here." These look more like in-house, Canaanite skirmishes.

Israel's beginnings are mysterious from an archaeological point of view, so we can't be dogmatic about explaining how and when Israel began. But it does seem that a nation eventually called "Israel" probably came on the scene gradually and relatively peacefully.

The Israelites were probably originally made up of a mixture of groups: an indigenous population of Canaanites and outsiders, likely nomads or others who wandered into this part of the world after Egyptian (to the south) and Hittite (to the north) decline left a power vacuum in the region. The destruction at Bethel and Hazor, then, isn't evidence for the "conquest" of Canaan from the outside, but probably of internal rebellion or some other type of conflict that ancient tribes couldn't keep from getting into.

So where did the biblical story of the conquest come from? Good question, and welcome to the world of biblical scholarship (though you still need your ID card and decoder ring for full membership). It seems that, as time went on and Israel became a nation (after 1000 BCE), stories of these earlier skirmishes grew and turned into exaggerated stories of Israel's wars against the Canaanites in days of old. These stories probably tell us more about Israel's later conflicts with the original population of the land (during the time of Israel's kings) than what happened centuries earlier. The presence of similar exaggerations, like we saw with King Mesha, supports this view.

That exact explanation may not be completely right, it's not a hill to die on, and we do need to keep an open mind. But it's a reasonable explanation given what we know at present. What most everyone is certain about, however, is that the Bible's version of events is not what happened.

And that puts the question "How could God have all those Canaanites put to death?" in a different light, indeed.

He didn't.

God Lets His Children Tell the Story

IF YOU ASK ME—and you have to because I am writing this book and I can do what I want—it's good news that the Canaanite extermination didn't happen. "How could God order the Israelites to do such a thing?" He didn't. The Israelites just said he did. Problem solved.

But not really. Another big question raises its head: Why would the Israelites write a story about God that isn't true—and what are we supposed to do today with a Holy Bible that makes up lies? At least that's how some might ask the question.

Still, it's a good question. So good, in fact, we're going to spend the whole next chapter talking about how the Israelites wrote about the past. But, for now, I just want to say, and I don't mean to keep harping on it, but, actually, I guess I do: *the ancient Israelites were an ancient tribal people.* They saw the world and their God in tribal ways. They told stories of their tribal past, led into battle by a tribal warrior God who valued the same things they did—like killing enemies and taking their land. This is how *they* connected with God—in their time, in their way.

I have to say, I'm a lot less bothered by a Bible that tells ancient stories than I am by the thought of God exterminating a population and giving their land to others.

Whatever we do, let's not imagine that the Israelites were ancient versions of ourselves, maybe less well groomed, who were "nice," read their Bibles daily, the kind you could invite to church and want to marry your daughter, who would vote Republican or drive a hybrid. We respect these biblical stories most when we try to understand what the writers did and why, not when we place false expectations on them, like seeing them as a timeless script or a permanent fixture for how to think about God.

But this raises an even deeper question, and I'll bet some of you were losing patience waiting for me to get there: If God, in whatever mysterious way we can imagine, is behind scripture—if the Bible is God's Holy Word—and if we, too, are to meet God in its pages, why would God allow himself to be cast in the role of a majorly hacked off tribal deity if he wasn't?

He's God, after all. Why does he even work with a script written from a violent and tribal mind-set? Why didn't God stop the storytellers? "No, sorry. Listen, I get the whole tribal thing. It's how you roll, but we're not going to do it that way. You have no idea how much trouble Richard Dawkins is going to cause with all this. Plus, Jesus is going to dismantle this 'kill your enemies and take their land' business. Best to avoid the problem altogether."

Instead of working within the system, God could have disallowed it. Then the Israelites could have written a wholly different kind of story altogether, a story no one had ever seen before, and knocked everyone's socks off. That's the kind of ancient storytelling I would have signed off on—if I were God.

But I'm not and I've given up trying to get into God's head, and I wish others would, too. Still, here is something that makes sense to me, a mystery that keeps staring me in the face every time I open my Bible and read it. The Bible—from back to front—is the story of God told from the limited point of view of real people living at a certain place and time.

It's not like the Israelites were debating whether or not to go ahead and describe God as a mighty warrior. They had no choice. That's just how it was done—that was their cultural language. And if the writers had somehow been able to step outside of their culture and invent a new way of talking, their story would have made no sense to anyone else.

The Bible looks the way it does because "God lets his children tell the story," so to speak.

Children see the world from their limited gaze. A second grader might give a class presentation on what mom does all day. She will talk about her mom from her point of view, rooted in love and devotion. She'll filter—unconsciously and in an age-appropriate manner—her mother's day through how she perceives her family and her role in the family. She'll get some things more or less correct, but she will also misunderstand other things, and get still other things plain wrong.

Or think of how young boys in the schoolyard talk about their fathers. There are ways of "telling the story of your father" that get the point across, to make sure everyone knows you have the best dad around.

I remember telling my friends in elementary school that my father was an engineer who left a promising academic career in Russia before coming to America after World War II. He also knew how to handle a rifle. There was "historical truth" in there, but you had to know where to look. My story reflected my context: I was a young boy in the schoolyard, following, for the most part without thinking, the unstated cultural rules for how these stories are told.

My father wasn't an engineer but a blue-collar machinist—I actually confused "engineer" with "machinist" because I didn't know what either was. I grew up a poor kid in a rich town, believing my dad was great and that he could match up with the suit-and-tie crowd. But he wore blue work clothes that smelled like machine oil and shaved metal. And he didn't leave a promising academic career. He was a good student (he always liked to remind me) through secondary school, and he wanted to be a schoolteacher. But Stalin took his parents' farm away, threw his father into a concentration camp, and, when World War II happened, he went off to war. He barely finished high school.

And as for the war, it was never an option in the schoolyard to give *all* the details. My father began on the Russian side and saw some action, but not much. He was soon captured by the Nazis and, being fluent in Russian and German, served out the rest of the war as a translator. Raised in a Mennonite home, he was a pacifist and didn't like to talk about the possibility that he may have killed someone. I saw him shoot a rifle once—he hit the bull's-eye and won a turkey. In my well-intentioned mind, I imagined him doing the same in battle. I filled in the gaps and he became a war hero.

And I definitely never mentioned to my schoolmates the many things my father did that were *actually* heroic but not quite as exciting for school-aged boys. My father rushed from his dirty job, without changing, to get to all my Little League games—and I always noticed how many of the fathers with suit-and-tie jobs never seemed to get there. He held me in the middle of the night catching my vomit in a napkin. He worked himself ragged weekend after weekend for months and years to turn our tattered and tiny house into something a bit nicer. He and my mom chose to put up some paneling in the basement for their bedroom so my sister and I could each have our own bedroom in our tiny house. He resigned himself to working long hours in an unfulfilling job he tolerated at best to make sure we had a roof over our heads, clothes on our backs, cars to drive, and the opportunity to go to college. (FYI, Mom gets a lot of credit, too.)

As I got older I was able to understand and articulate all this. But as a young boy in a schoolyard culture, the truer and bigger picture of my father wasn't on my radar screen. And if it had been, had I talked like that, it would have ruined me. I might as well have just told them my dad played with dolls and wore a skirt. I was proud of my dad. I believed he really was the best, and I made sure my friends knew it. I was a storyteller.

I think at least parts of the Bible work something like that. It may be hard—sometimes impossible—to see the history in Israel's stories, but we do get a good picture of how these ancient Israelites *experienced God*.

Reading the Bible responsibly and respectfully today means learning what it meant for ancient Israelites to talk about God the way they did, and not pushing alien expectations onto texts written long ago and far away.

*   *   *

Christians—as well as Jews—over the centuries have had to come to terms with this tribal portrait of God and have moved on; the ancient tribal description of God is *not the last word*.

Speaking for Christians, capturing land and holding on to it by violence is not a gospel way of living. Christians today, therefore, have an obligation *not* to "follow the Bible" here, not to allow the ancient tribal description of God in the Old Testament to be the last word.

These ancient writers had an adequate understanding of God *for them in their time*, but not *for all time*—and if we take that to heart, we will actually be in a better position to respect these ancient voices and see what they have to say rather than whitewashing the details and making up "explanations" to ease our stress.

And for Christians, the gospel has always been the lens through which Israel's stories are read—which means, for Christians, Jesus, not the Bible, has the final word.

The story of God's people has moved on, and so must we.

Why This Chapter Is So Important and So Dreadfully Long

I MADE CANAANITE EXTERMINATION the first big issue of this book, and took my sweet time about it, too. Here's why.

First, if I had to give a top-three list of awkward issues that trouble Christian readers of the Bible, God ordering, sanctioning, or carrying out mass killings in the Old Testament is on it—often at the top. God definitely has violent moments in the New Testament, namely how Jesus is tortured and then executed on a cross. And the book of Revelation has more than enough wrath and violence, including one scene with blood up to a horse's eyeballs flowing down a street for two hundred miles.

But most Christians instinctively understand that Jesus's crucifixion—although raising its own issues of God's violence—isn't the same thing as exterminating a population to take their land, and that the book of Revelation is off-the-charts weird and, of all the books of the Bible, is definitely not meant to be read literally—or to use scholar talk, it "participates in the exaggerated and violent rhetoric of ancient apocalyptic thought." Memorize that sentence and people will instantly want to know you and lend you money.

I have found that sincere readers of the Bible are much more bothered by   and have a more difficult time defending to themselves and others— God's seemingly over-the-top knee-jerk violence in the Old Testament, and especially Canaanite extermination, which some contemporary atheists hail as exhibit A for the utter stupidity of any faith in the God of the Bible.

The second reason we camped out with Canaanite extermination is that it drives home a key point for understanding many other parts of the Old Testament: the ancient Israelites' tribal mentality about themselves, their world, and their God is reflected in what they wrote. That's not bad, that's not good. It just is what it is. Getting a handle on that paves the way for understanding other issues in the Old Testament that make us do a double take.

Israel's ancient ways don't always pose problems for modern readers. We can get our arms around the biblical metaphor of God as a shepherd, even if we don't really get all the nuances of shepherding in the ancient world. We generally get what it means for God to be a king, even though most Americans have neither served nor seen one, except on TV when British royalty get married. But kings today are still light-years away from what ancient tribal warrior-kings were like. Still, making a connection between then and now isn't a huge stretch, and few pace the floor at night thinking about it.

But parts of the Old Testament have a weirdness factor that often crosses over to uh-oh moments for readers today, like: God has a lot of literal, audible conversations back and forth with people, especially early on in the Bible, like it's not really a big deal.

Animals talk, too—twice: a serpent talks to Eve in the Garden of Eden and a donkey engages a prophet named Balaam in an extended back-and-forth. I don't think for one minute that ancient Israelites thought animals could talk. They knew the power of stories and used them. Though that idea doesn't sit well with those who have a rulebook expectation of the Bible. They simply assume that if the Bible says animals talked, they talked. End of discussion.

Yet, if even the most sincere among them heard someone say, "Yeah, God appeared to me this morning. We talked. He gave me specific instructions of how I can obey him better. Rex stopped chewing his bone long enough to add his two cents, and he also was able to work in that question about the eternal destiny of the neighbor's cat that he's been dying to ask."—well, they'd sprint down the street while calling 911.

Moving on, and more to the point, you may have noticed that the Old Testament contains a lot of laws. Laws are necessary: societies can't function without them. And some of Israel's laws make sense to us, roll off our tongues naturally, and don't give Christians a minute's stress: don't steal, kill, commit adultery—that sort of thing.

But it's hard to know what to do with other laws, or how God could ever have been responsible for them.

If a virgin daughter is seduced, the seducer must marry her and give the father the "bride-price for virgins." In the ancient world, this law functioned to protect the nonvirgin woman from winding up without a husband and becoming destitute or a prostitute (your two main options for unmarried nonvirgins). The father could still refuse the marriage, but in that case the seducer *still* has to pay him the bride-price. Why? Because his daughter is his "property" and damaged goods. Dad gets paid, regardless.

Other laws are also hard for Christians to get on board with: don't eat pork or lobster, and stone to death persistently rebellious sons (OK, maybe we can relate to that). The list of sacrifice laws that specify when, how often, for what reason, and what kind of animal is as exciting to read as instructions for filling out a Schedule C.

When you come up against these laws and you're tempted to skip them, mutilate the pages, or spiral down into an existential crisis, remember— and I apparently do not grow tired of saying it—that ancient tribal culture is not like ours.

Also remember that, even though these laws were real and sincere means by which Israel connected with God, the fact that they are in the

Bible doesn't mean they are automatically timeless and have permanent staying power. This would be placing a false expectation on the Bible.

Judaism has its own long, rich, and diverse history of working out how these ancient laws *needed* to have fresh meaning in new contexts (as we'll see in chapter 6). Sacrifice laws, for example, can only be obeyed in the temple in Jerusalem. But once Jews fled their homeland after the Romans razed the temple and massacred much of the Jewish population in 70 CE, Judaism has had to work through the implications.

Christians have taken another route. They have re-evaluated these laws against the backdrop of the Gospels and the letters of the apostle Paul, which give Christians a different picture of how these laws work or are cancelled out after the first Easter Sunday. For Christians, this re-evaluation is a *necessary* thought process: not a show of disrespect for these parts of the Old Testament to discard them like junk mail, but an acknowledgement that Israel's laws reflect the ancient times and are not permanent (more on this in chapter 6).

The "science" of the biblical writers was also ancient. Creatures didn't evolve but were made by God as we see them, like a potter molding clay, in male and female pairs. The world was flat, probably a round disk, created by God a few short thousand years ago after holding at bay a watery chaos. Above the earth was a solid dome of some sort, held up by pillars (mountains), that held back the "waters above" (hence, the *blue* sky). Above it all was God's throne, and beneath the earth was the shadowy, nondescript abode of the dead called "Sheol." (We'll revisit this ancient map of the cosmos in chapter 3.)

We understand today that the physical universe is bigger and older and operates very differently than how the biblical writers, and all other ancient people, thought. Many Christians stumble over this, thinking they are showing respect for the Bible and obeying God by making the biblical story mesh with modern science, or rejecting modern science entirely in favor of God's Word.

But there is no need to feel embarrassed or unfaithful by acknowledging that ancient writers wrote from an ancient mind-set. When ancient Israelites wrote as they did about the physical world, they were expressing their faith in God in ways that fit their understanding. It shouldn't get our knickers in a twist to admit that, from a scientific point of view, they were wrong. That doesn't make their faith or the God behind it all any less genuine.

So that's why this chapter looks the way it does—to put right in front of our eyes the antiquity of the Bible, and to see how embracing that antiquity is the *beginning* point for exploring the Bible as it is, to accept the challenge to investigate even some of its darker pathways, and so to begin learning how we, too, can embrace Israel's story for our journey.

Israel's *story*. That's really what this comes down to. Canaanite genocide is part of Israel's story of the past—not a historical account of something God did.

In that sense, Canaanite genocide is more than just a perplexing moral *problem* to work through. It has a positive value, for it is a *window* onto a much larger issue, one that we face on virtually every page of the Bible and that we are going to look at next: How do biblical writers talk about the past?

God Likes Stories

What Happened?

THE FILM *42* depicts the story of Jackie Robinson breaking the Major League Baseball color barrier with the Brooklyn Dodgers in 1947. I am a baseball nerd, and the Robinson story is compelling and moving. I was eager to see how the film would handle one scene in particular that hits me every time: Dodgers' owner Branch Rickey's explanation of what drove him to stick his neck out and introduce a black player to a heretofore wholly white world.

According to the film, Robinson asks Rickey several times why he did it, but never got a straight answer. One day, Rickey finally told him, a bit reluctantly, of the time decades earlier when he was coaching the Ohio Wesleyan University baseball team. Their black star first baseman, Charles "Tommy" Thomas, had suffered all sorts of racial onslaughts, which moved Rickey deeply and motivated him to bring justice to the game.

My mind went immediately to the same scene in Ken Burns's magisterial—nay, celestial—PBS documentary *Baseball,* which I've watched so often I should be listed in the credits (and I intend to follow up my phone calls with a strongly worded letter). Here we see this episode through the eyes of Red Barber, the legendary Brooklyn Dodgers' radio announcer.

Rickey confided to Barber that he had been tormented for decades by an image of what occurred after a specific game in Kentucky. Racist taunts and abuse were taking their toll on Thomas. He was sitting on his hotel bed, tears falling to the floor, rubbing his hands as if to tear the skin off the bones. "Black skin, . . . black skin. If I could only make 'em white."

That's powerful enough, but on top of that, to see Barber, raised in the racist South, recall that moment decades later, in his twilight years, clearly acknowledging the deep debt of gratitude he had to Rickey for changing his own world—well, it just gets to me. I feel shame about the game that has played such a big part in my life, but I'm also—not to sound trite— inspired by the story of redemption and a vision for me to do better in not turning a blind eye to gross injustice.

As you've guessed, the Ken Burns version speaks to me and the film version left me sort of flat. But that's just me. Someone else might feel differently.

Either way—and now I'm getting to my point—neither version gets it completely "right." Both versions are *interpretations* of what happened in the late 1940s in the life of Jackie Robinson. They tell that story differently because they are *stories*.

I don't mean "stories" like Hansel and Gretel, which are not attempts to present the past—at least every terrified five-year-old hopes not. I just mean that these two versions of the "Robinson story" are more than a laundry list of facts strung together accurately. They each weave together bits and pieces of the past into narratives that reflect how the two different storytellers—in this case a dramatic film producer and a documentarian— want to tell the story to inspire and inform.

The Robinson story could be told from other angles. As a shrewd businessman, Rickey was probably thinking of the fact that black players meant black ticket-buyers and more revenue. He might also have realized that bringing talented black players to Major League Baseball would yield a higher level of play, something observers had known for decades from watching players in the Negro League. Some might add, with some cyni- cism, that Rickey was a consummate showman who needed to be center stage any way he could. All these angles would be legitimate ways of tell-ing the Robinson story. None would be "wrong."

Stories of the past differ because storytellers are human beings. No storyteller is all knowing about the past, but limited by his or her own time and place, and the fact that no human sees every angle of everything.

Stories also differ by what storytellers are consciously trying to "do" in their stories, what their takeaway is. They are not objective observers and don't pretend to be. They are artists bringing past and present together to leave the audience with something to ponder, to persuade—to inspire. (Actually, I am also framing this book's material according to my goal: to show Christians that the "Bible as rulebook" is a human invention and not what God intended or wants. My goal explains how I present and organize this material.)

To do their thing, storytellers "shape" the past. They decide what to include, what order to put things in, how to compress or combine scenes to save time and get to the money shot, and so on. They also invent dia-logue and scenes to knit the narrative together. They have to, since much of the past is inaccessible to storytellers—they themselves weren't there to see and hear what happened.

And even if they were, the past is a fragile thing. It is never just "there" waiting for us to press replay. The past lies in our memories and the memo-ries of others, dormant, in bits and pieces, waiting to be gathered together into a story to be told. Recalling the past is actually never simply a process of *remembering* but of *creating* a narrative out of discrete, imperfect memories (our own or those of others), woven together into a narrative thread that is deeply influenced by how we see ourselves and our world here and now.

All attempts to put the past into words are *interpretations* of the past, not "straight history." There is no such thing. Anywhere.

Including the Bible.

The biblical storytellers recall the past, often the very distant past, not "objectively," but purposefully. They had skin in the game. These were *their* stories. They wove *narratives* of the past to give meaning to their present—to persuade, motivate, and inspire.

To make that happen, like all storytellers, biblical storytellers invented and augmented dialogue, characters, and scenes to turn past moments into a flowing story—not because they were lazy or sneaky, but because that's what all storytellers need to do to create a narrative. They shifted and arranged the past, or wove together discrete moments, all for the purpose of telling *their* story for *their* audience.

The Bible itself gives 100 percent proof that the biblical writers were doing just that: they present the same past events from different perspectives. And by different, I mean *very* different—big scenes, important details, and dialogue differ among writers.

The story of Jesus, the center of the Christian faith, is told from four different perspectives in the four Gospels. In the Old Testament we have two lengthy, very different, takes on Israel's past. At times these stories of Jesus and Israel contradict each other. They can't be combined somehow to make one story without losing large portions of any one of these stories. Each story is meant to stand on its own—as their storytellers intended them to.

What could be more normal than for different people, living at different times, in different places, who wrote about the past for different reasons and to different audiences, to produce different versions on the past? Nothing. And that's what we see in the Bible.

Readers who come to the Bible expecting something more like an accurate textbook, a more-or-less objective recalling of the past—because, surely, God wouldn't have it any other way—are in for an uncomfortable read. But if they take seriously the words in front of them, they will quickly find that the Bible doesn't deliver on that expectation. Not remotely.

Expecting the Bible to act out of character leads to stress and anxiety and leaves us with a choice: either change our expectations to conform to what is actually in the Bible or find some way to force the Bible into our mold.

I'm going with the first option.

When we allow the Bible to set its own agenda, to show us what we have the right to expect—trusting God enough to let the Bible be what it is—we open ourselves to God's Word with its challenges and possibilities without a lurking fear of what we might find and going into shock when we find it.

What drove the Bible's storytellers to recall the past the way they did was the quest to experience God in the present, a sometimes volatile and catastrophic present.

What makes the Bible God's Word isn't its uncanny historical accuracy, as some insist, but the sacred experiences these stories point to, beyond the words themselves. Watching these ancient pilgrims work through their faith, even wrestling with how they did that, models for us our own journeys of seeking to know God better and commune with him more deeply.

If we miss that—if we expect the Bible to be God's objective Spark Notes on the past—the stories in the Bible will forever be a source of needless frustration.

To see this in action, let's begin by asking Jesus, well, by asking at least the people who wrote about him.

The Stories of Jesus

THAT'S "STORIES." PLURAL.

The Bible contains four Gospels, four stories of Jesus, four very different stories. So different, in fact, that if you think that they merely report historical facts, get ready for one massive headache.

The basic overview of Jesus's life is similar in all four Gospels: some early episodes of Jesus's public life, gathering of the disciples, some teachings, conflicts with some of the Jewish leaders, his arrest, trial, execution, and resurrection. But when we get to the details, you wonder why these four writers couldn't have done a better job of staying on the same page and saved us all a few sleepless nights.

After all, we're talking about the *life of Jesus* here, *the* central point of the Christian story! Let's get it right, shall we?

But we find that each Gospel writer tells the story of Jesus in his own way. That's why we say, "The Gospel *according to* Matthew," and so on. *According to* . . . yes, exactly. That says it all.

The Gospels differ because their writers lived at different times and places and wrote for different reasons decades after Jesus lived. Each writer produced his own portrait of Jesus that captured the faith of the community he wrote for.

The Gospels are also anonymous, and the names attached to them come to us from early church tradition. Likely none was an eyewitness.

The writers relied on stories of Jesus that were circulating orally, perhaps (or probably) going back to what eyewitnesses had seen.

The Gospel writers also clearly relied on each other—at least the first three—Matthew, Mark, and Luke. For example, most of Mark's Gospel (90 percent or so) finds its way into Matthew, whereas Luke only carries over about 50 percent of Mark. Both Matthew and Luke use Mark but differently.

Also (if you like statistics) Matthew and Luke are connected to each other in ways that leave Mark out of the picture: Matthew and Luke share about 25 percent of their stories with each other, but not with Mark.

That's enough math. Ferreting out exactly how Matthew, Mark, and Luke depend on each other is the stuff of serious scholarly books with an excitement value that makes *Meet the Press* look like *Star Wars*. But no one doubts that these Gospel writers were working off one another somehow.

And here is the point that I can't stress enough: even though Matthew, Mark, and Luke are *clearly consciously* connected to one another somehow, each Gospel writer also *clearly* has no problem whatsoever going off and telling the story of Jesus in his own unique way.

I think it's worth taking a moment and letting that last point sink in.

Matthew and Luke used Mark as a base (as many scholars agree), but then they kept right on going and felt perfectly free to add to and adjust Mark's story of Jesus to make their own versions. And the overlap between Matthew and Luke means that one of them may have used the other—and kept right on changing things to suit him. Luke's Gospel even begins by mentioning that "many" have written their own accounts of Jesus, and that he was sifting through a lot of information to get his version down.

That should tell us something about what it meant for biblical writers to "write history." Getting the past "right" in a modern sense wasn't high priority. All four Gospels are connected to history, but each also tells us a lot about *how these writers saw Jesus,* what they believed about him, what was important to them and their communities. Judging where history ends and creative writing begins is tough, and biblical scholars go back and forth on all that (usually politely but now and then armed and loaded).

Then we have the Gospel of John, the odd man out. John's story of Jesus is so out of step with the others that it is sometimes hard to see how he could be talking about the same person.

He leaves out most things the other Gospels include (Jesus's baptism, his temptation in the wilderness, parables, exorcisms, and concern for the poor) and adds long speeches and episodes that are nowhere to be found in the others (like Jesus was with God at creation, Jesus claimed to be "one" with the Father, turning water to wine, raising his friend Lazarus from the dead, and a long prayer for his disciples in the "upper room" before his crucifixion). In Matthew, Mark, and Luke, Jesus's default teaching method is to use parables. In John, Jesus never teaches in parables.

One story highlights John's unique take on Jesus: where Jesus goes to the temple and turns over tables, makes a whip, and hauls off on everybody. Frankly, if Jesus did this sort of thing more often, maybe throw in a chariot chase scene or two, more kids would read the Bible, but let's not get sidetracked.

John's version doesn't line up with the other three. John not only includes dialogue missing in the other three Gospels, but he also places the scene at an entirely different point in his story—at the *beginning* of Jesus's public life, right after he changed the water to wine at the wedding at Cana (which the other Gospels don't mention, by the way). In Matthew, Mark, and Luke, this scene happens near the *end* of Jesus's life, a few days before his crucifixion.

One can't be dogmatic about it, but Matthew, Mark, and Luke are likely following the flow of history more than John. Jesus might not have lasted as long as he did as a public figure had wreaking havoc on the temple been his opening move. Bursting into the temple and throwing tables around is asking for trouble—like yelling "bomb" in a police station or burning an American flag on the White House lawn. You'd attract a lot of negative attention, which is what we see in Matthew, Mark, and Luke; Jesus was arrested and executed a few days later.

John is deliberately shaping the past, and not apologizing for it. He moved this temple episode to the beginning of *his* story of Jesus and lengthened it to include a debate with the religious leaders. Why? Because, more than the other three Gospel writers, John is big on Jesus's divine authority over the religious leaders. That's part of his agenda, and so he shapes the past to make the point.

The fact that John makes a move like this doesn't mean his Gospel is a shoddy piece of work and the other three Gospels are better because they are more "accurate." None of the Gospels can be judged like that. All four are shaped presentations of Jesus's life, even down to some basic episodes, such as the following.

Little Baby Jesuses

THE STORIES OF JESUS'S BIRTH are great places to see how the Gospel writers shape the past.

For starters, Mark and John don't even bother bringing it up, like it's a detail we can do without. Matthew and Luke, however, think Jesus's birth is a big deal—and by big deal I mean that whole part where the Spirit of God "overshadows" Mary and Jesus is conceived without Joseph's help.

That sounds like an important detail to mention: Jesus doesn't have a human father. You'd think for any Gospel writer this would be his lead. But Mark and John pass, and a lot of readers have been left wondering why. Had this part of the Jesus story just not reached their ears yet? Or perhaps Matthew and Luke were the innovators, adding something to the Jesus story others hadn't?

We're not going to solve this one here, and we don't need to. All I'm saying is that the absence of this episode in two of the four Gospels is a huge signal that their stories of Jesus are *significantly* different, even in key details, and that the differences are real and deep and need to be respected not ignored.

The details of Matthew's and Luke's birth stories are familiar to any parent or child who has ever been part of a "Christmas pageant," with its blatant violations of child labor laws in the weeks of round-the-clock rehearsals leading up to Christmas—but I digress. Even though Matthew and Luke both include a birth story, their versions are so different you couldn't blame an innocent reader for concluding they are talking about two different births.

The part about the Magi (a.k.a. "wise men") following the star and visiting baby Jesus is only in Matthew. Same with King Herod killing all the boy babies in order to make sure he takes out Jesus, too, which never quite makes it into the Christmas pageants. (If your church ever decides to hand swords to ten-year-olds, please e-mail me. I'll adjust my schedule to come watch the chaos.) The same goes for baby Jesus and his parents escaping to Egypt to steer clear of that threat.

Why doesn't Luke include these scenes? They weren't worth his time? He didn't know about them? Did Matthew have his own private pipeline of information he tapped into?

Scholars disagree on a good many things, but most think Matthew probably created at least some of these scenes to shape his story. A star— millions of light-years away—can't actually move and then stop over one specific house on earth, nor do stars even appear to do so from our earthly vantage point. Herod's massacre of children isn't hinted at in any other ancient source of the day, which also rouses some suspicion over whether it happened.

So is Matthew a liar? Is that what we're supposed to think? Only if you grade Matthew along with the other Gospel writers by a standard they clearly weren't operating under.

Matthew's portrait of Jesus serves his purpose: he drops into his Gospel images of Jesus that remind you of *Moses and the exodus story*. So a guiding star is like the pillar of fire that guided the Israelites to safety across the Red Sea. Herod's edict to kill the children and Jesus's escape is like Pharaoh's edict to throw the male infants into the Nile with baby Moses escaping. Jesus's trek down into Egypt as an infant and then back home again echoes Moses's and later Israel's journeys to and from Egypt.

We'll come back later to Matthew's connecting of Jesus and Moses.

Here we need to focus on a different question: Is Matthew reporting history as we understand the word? Did all these things happen? I am committed to keeping an open mind, but, along with most scholars, I think not in this case. And even phrasing the question that way, as important as it may seem to us, won't help us understand what Matthew is doing.

Matthew intentionally, creatively, connects Jesus to Moses, because this is Matthew's way of deeply connecting Jesus to Israel's story. By making Jesus "Moses 2.0" he is telling his readers that Jesus needs to be understood not at a distance from Israel's story, but as God's way of taking Israel's story to the next, climactic stage with Jesus at the center *rather than* Moses.

The part about angels announcing Jesus's birth to the shepherds (think Linus in *A Charlie Brown Christmas*) only happens in Luke's version. The same with the announcement of John the Baptist's birth to Mary's relative, Elizabeth, and Mary paying her a visit to compare pregnancies. Also, in Luke, the angel announces to Mary that she will bear Jesus. In Matthew, Joseph gets that message.

Whether Luke created these scenes or they are traditions that, for some unknown reason, he alone records, he is nevertheless, like Matthew, shaping his story of Jesus—though differently.

Luke's Jesus is very "kingly" right from the start. A heavenly announcement at Jesus's birth, which is "good news" and brings "peace," echoes how Romans talked about the birth of Caesar Augustus, the Caesar at Jesus's birth. Luke's birth story is portraying Jesus, not Caesar, as king of the world.

Mary's song of praise to God about her miraculous pregnancy would have sounded *very* familiar to those who knew the story of David. In the Old Testament the childless Hannah gave birth miraculously to a son, Samuel, who would grow up to anoint David as king. Hannah's song of thanksgiving to God looks forward to the time when, with David as king, God would humble the proud and arrogant, and exalt the lowly and humble. Mary praises God for the child in her womb for exactly the same reasons.

Pairing Hannah and Mary is Luke's way of saying, "Think David when you think of Jesus." Jesus is David revisited—Israel's rightful king.

We'll hit these birth stories, especially Luke's, from another angle in chapter 6. For now, we only need to see that Luke and Matthew clearly crafted two very different birth stories. I understand that it may be hard for some to think of biblical writers adding to, adjusting, and even creating portions of the life of Jesus as they see fit, but think of it another way.

Perhaps by the time they wrote their Gospels, some forty years after Jesus's life, after the resurrection, the bigness of it all, not fully grasped at first, had begun to come into its own. Perhaps over time the Gospel writers *had* to create scenes of guiding stars and angelic choirs in retrospect to get the *real* Jesus across, the Jesus they were coming to understand.

So what I mean by the *real* Jesus is not any one of the four Gospels getting Jesus more right, nor is it mashing them together to make a hybrid of what Jesus said and did. Actually, very early in the history of the church, in the second century CE, a theologian named Tatian thought it might be a good idea to do just that, to combine these four Gospels into one super-Gospel. You can guess what happened: to pull it off, he had to smooth over contradictions between them, rearrange the order of events, and generally obliterate any notion of the four-ness of the Gospels.

Although it caught on for a while in some places, Tatian's work wound up not having a long shelf life. Wiser heads prevailed. All four Gospels had to be respected as they are, and what God has rent asunder, let no one join together.

To ferret out what may or may not have "actually" happened if we had been following Jesus around and call *that* the "real" Jesus is not only a completely unreasonable quest, but also misses the point.

Christians believe by faith that the real Jesus is the Jesus of the full story—the resurrected Jesus. That Jesus was not and could not have been understood by walking with Jesus in and around Galilee. The disciples themselves—those Jesus handpicked to carry on his work—were utterly clueless about the big picture.

The real Jesus can only be truly understood from a later vantage point—interpreted after the resurrection when the broader implications of who Jesus was and what he did could be better grasped. That is the Jesus the Gospel writers give us, each in his own way.

That's where I land, but I'm just riffing, and if it's not convincing to you, leave it to the side and work it out some other way. We're all free to put the pieces together as we think best. The bigger point here is that the stories of Jesus's birth behave the way stories do, and we can't wish that away.

We see the same diverse portraits of Jesus when we move to the other end of his life.

Who Saw the Big Moment?

THE END OF JESUS'S STORY, namely what happens Easter morning, is reported very differently by the Gospel writers. Even at the climactic and *central* moment in the story—Jesus walking out of his burial tomb—the Gospel writers are on different pages.

Matthew alone reports that Roman soldiers were ordered to guard the tomb to make sure no one stole the body to fake the resurrection. After Jesus is raised, we read that the Jewish leaders pay off the soldiers to say they were asleep at the post and Jesus's body was stolen. This story, unique as it is to Matthew, reads like it was created by Matthew as a slam against the unbelieving Jewish leaders, like other episodes sprinkled through Matthew's Gospel.

And who shows up at the tomb to find it empty? According to Matthew, it was Mary Magdalene and the "other Mary" (possibly Jesus's mother), who are greeted by an earthquake and an angel telling them what happened. Then Jesus appears to the two women and they run off to tell the disciples.

Luke's version has a veritable women's club meeting at the tomb to anoint Jesus's body with spices: Mary Magdalene, Joanna, Mary the mother of Jesus, and the "other women." They see not one angel, but "two men" (angels, I guess) who tell them what happened—but no earthquake. They run off to tell the other disciples, and Peter comes running back to see for himself. Only later does Jesus appear to all the disciples at once.

Mark's Gospel has two (maybe more) endings, which complicates things—an original shorter ending and a longer one added in the second century (probably), to make it look more like the other three Gospels (probably).

In the shorter ending, Mary Magdalene, Mary the mother of James, and Solome come to the tomb to anoint Jesus's body. They see the rock to the tomb rolled away and a "young man" (one, not two) sitting there who tells them what happened. They are frightened, so they run away, telling no one (though in one of the possible later additions they tell Peter and others). The End.

The longer ending to Mark rewinds a bit and now Jesus appears only to Mary Magdalene. She tells the others, but they don't believe her until Jesus starts appearing to them himself. Jesus also appears to two men along the road (as in Luke), and then commissions the disciples to "go into all the world and proclaim the good news to the whole creation" (as in Matthew). Looks like whoever added these parts might have been using Luke and Matthew as guides.

John's story is different still. Mary Magdalene goes to the tomb alone, then runs back to get Peter and "the other disciple" (John). These two have a footrace to the tomb—the writer feeling the need to tell us that "the other disciple" gets there first and "saw and believed." Still, the disciples seem to be generally clueless about what is going on—no angel or young man/men are there to tell them what happened, just . . . wow, it's empty. At this point Jesus appears to Mary Magdalene, who has trouble recognizing him at first. Next, Jesus passes through a solid wall to surprise his disciples, who are huddled in fear that their lives might be in danger, too.

John's Gospel also records more appearances, including the famous scene with "doubting Thomas," who won't believe Jesus is alive unless he can see for himself.

This story is one of many reasons scholars think that John's Gospel was likely written later than the others, about sixty years or so after Jesus's lifetime. After Thomas is convinced Jesus in the flesh is actually standing in front of him, Jesus says, "Have you believed because you have seen? *Blessed are those who have not seen and yet have come to believe.*" The earlier generation that knew Jesus was dying out. John probably added these words to encourage faith in a generation removed from the founding generation.

If we are fixed on the Bible as a book that has to get history "right," the Gospels become a crippling problem. And think about the implications of claiming that the Bible, to be worthy of the name, *has* to get history right. Just read the Gospels. They clearly give us very different portraits of Jesus. Did God not get the memo about the kind of Bible Christians "need" to have?

Or are we saying that God intended one, clean, accurate version of the story, but turned his back for a minute, the Gospel writers went nuts, and now we're left with a mess to clean up? (Which reminds me of a cartoon I saw on Facebook, where Jesus is teaching a large crowd and he tells them to pay attention, because he doesn't want "like four versions of this going around." Facebook teaches us so much.)

Starting with the wrong assumptions actually devalues the Bible that we have by wanting something else. But God seems to be in the habit of working through normal channels, and the Gospel writers were normal storytellers of that time and of any time—they offered their *perspective.* Maybe this isn't a problem to be solved or avoided, but just more evidence of how God rolls.

The Gospels model a lesson that has been repeated again and again throughout the history of Christianity: followers of Jesus always have and always will meet Jesus and see *him* from where *they* are and they will experience Jesus differently as a result.

And maybe God is just fine with that. In fact, it seems he's been fine with it long before the time of Jesus.

The Stories of Israel

JUST AS THE NEW TESTAMENT contains four stories of Jesus, the Old Testament contains two stories of Israel's period of the monarchy, the roughly six hundred years from Israel's first (and disastrous) king, Saul (around 1100-ish BCE), to the end of the monarchy when the Babylonians sacked the capital city of Jerusalem in 586 BCE.

The earlier version of the story is found in the books of 1 and 2 Samuel and 1 and 2 Kings. The second version is in 1 and 2 Chronicles, which in Christian Bibles follows immediately after 2 Kings—and that placement has proved to be a huge hurdle for readers to leap over.

If you've ever made it all the way through the long (and I don't mind saying repetitive) stories in Samuel and Kings, you're a trouper. Go out and buy yourself a little something nice. But then you turn the page to 1 Chronicles, and you probably did what any normal person with a busy schedule and an operating cerebral cortex would do: you skipped it. What are they trying to pull here? You just got done reading this in Samuel/ Kings. It's like chewing the same piece of steak twice.

No one blames you. I certainly don't. I blame early Bible editors, before the time of Jesus, probably.

Chronicles was originally placed toward the end, if not at *the* end, of the Old Testament—where it remains to this day in the Jewish Bible. But early on some editors (who even back then got in the way of good

writing)* got the bright idea of sticking Chronicles right after Samuel/
Kings—probably to group similar books together. The early Christians
went with that order, and these poor books have been trying to get
noticed ever since. The fact that Chronicles was known back then by the
title "The Things Left Over" didn't exactly encourage people to read it. (In
Greek it's *paraleipomenon*—pa-ra-lay-po-MEN-on. If you're looking for a
different kind of biblical-sounding name for your kids, look no further.)

Placing Chronicles after Kings was an inexcusably dumb move, if you
ask me, and I think God should give this editor some sort of temporary
afterlife punishment before entering his glory—like make him read the
entire *Left Behind* series nonstop for a year . . . out of order.

Forgive the rant, but the shame of it all is that Chronicles isn't mopping
up what's left over from Samuel/Kings. *It was intentionally crafted to give a
very different take on Israel's past.* That poor book is jumping up and down,
demanding to be read on its own terms, not treated like Samuel/Kings'
annoying little brother.

And when we do pay attention to Chronicles, we will get a crash course
on how Israel's ancient storytellers handled the past.

The two stories differ because they were written at different times to
answer different questions.

Samuel/Kings was written while the Israelites were in exile in Babylon
(sixth century BCE) and probably edited and updated sometime after they came
back to the land (late sixth to fifth century BCE). The pressing question for this
writer was, "How did we end up in Babylon, in exile from our homeland,
when we thought God would stick with us no matter what? What did we do
to deserve it?" They were trying to wrap their heads around what happened.

Chronicles was written much later, two hundred years or so, probably
sometime in the fourth century BCE at least, after the Israelites had been

---

* It goes without saying, of course, that the editors of *this* book are an angelic exception to
this tendency, and I would never, not in a million years, and on advice from my lawyer,
dream of suggesting anything to the contrary.

back in the land for generations. This writer's question wasn't "What did we do to deserve this?" but "After all this time, are we still the people of God? Is God ever going to show up and fix this mess? What is our future? Do we *have* a future?"

These two agendas are galaxies apart, and they yielded two *profoundly* different stories of Israel's monarchy.

Both versions agree that Israel began as a united kingdom, with Saul, then David, and then Solomon on the throne. After Solomon's reign, however, somewhere around 930 BCE, the nation had a political dispute over labor and taxes (as we see in 1 Kings) and split into the northern and southern kingdoms. Henceforth, the north was referred to by several names, the two most common were (confusingly) "Israel" and "Ephraim," the name of the main tribe that made up the northern kingdom. The south would be referred to as "Judah," the name of the main southern tribe.

Eventually, the northern kingdom would meet its end in 722 BCE when the mighty Assyrians captured the capital of Samaria and relocated much of its population to Assyria. The southern kingdom of Judah remained intact, more or less, for another 136 years until 586 BCE, when the Babylonians destroyed Jerusalem and the temple and took much of the population captive to Babylon.

My point is that each kingdom, north and south, had its own line of kings. The books of 1 and 2 Kings deal with *all of them,* but the Chronicles author leaves the northern kings out of his story.

Did he think no one would notice? Was he rushing to meet his deadline? No. He focused solely on the kings of the southern kingdom, the kingdom that went into Babylonian exile *and came back*—*his* people. By the time he wrote his version, the northern kingdom was already a distant memory, erased from the world scene by the Assyrians three hundred or so years earlier. Judah is all that's left and all that matters. Judah is the future.

So, as for differences, we can start by saying Chronicles leaves out half the picture—which is pretty selective storytelling. It's like a southerner telling the story of the United States and never venturing north of the Mason-Dixon Line.

And even in those places where Chronicles and Samuel/Kings cover the same exact ground, we almost always get very different points of view. For example, both versions have a scene where the prophet Nathan meets with King David (Israel is still one nation here) to give him the good news that God is absolutely on his side.

According to 2 Samuel, God makes David this promise:

> **Your** house and **your** king will endure forever before me. **Your** throne will be established forever.

That means David's dynasty (his house), beginning with his son Solomon, will continue unbroken for a very long time (which is what "forever" means in Hebrew, not literally "eternity").

The writer of 1 Chronicles puts different words into Nathan's mouth:

> I will set him over **my** house and **my** kingdom forever; his throne will be established forever.

What was *David's* dynasty in 2 Samuel ("your") now becomes *God's* dynasty in 1 Chronicles ("my").

You might think, "What's the big deal? Does it really matter whether Nathan said *your throne* or *my throne*?" Yes. Yes, it does.

For the writer of 2 Samuel, an unbroken line of descendants through David's son Solomon is still on the table—hence "*your* [David's] throne will be established forever." But by the time we get to 1 Chronicles, that unbroken line had been long gone for many generations. We can imagine the Judahites might have wondered whether the long dead line of David was a sign that God had indeed given up on them by now.

But the writer of Chronicles says, "No. You see, it's not really *David's* dynasty, anyway. It's God's. Times have been hard for us, no doubt. We still don't have a son of David on his rightful throne in Jerusalem, and we can't wait for that to happen. But we shouldn't get discouraged about that, or lose focus on the truly big picture. When all is said and done, it's really *God's* throne and he'll get it done—in time."

Expending energy to clean up this little mess and make both versions report Nathan's words the same way is not only futile (just read the words, for heaven's sake), but misses an important lesson to be learned here. Nathan's prophecy is just one small example in one verse that illustrates a big principle: these stories are not giving us history "straight" but history as the writers see it—better, history as they want their readers (which now includes us) to see it.

They weren't trying to pull a fast one, nor were they sloppy. That's modern thinking relying on modern rules of history writing. These two biblical storytellers shaped the past—*created* it to a certain extent—because their *present* circumstances demanded it.

You might even say, for these writers, the past *serves the needs of the present*.

And I think I just did.

The Past Serves the Present

A CLOSER LOOK at David and his son Solomon shows us how our two writers spun their careers in almost opposite ways to serve the needs of their presents.

In 2 Samuel, David's life looks like a Jerry Springer outtake. He's a great king and all, but we have this little episode where . . . uh . . . how do I put it . . . he has the honorable soldier Uriah assigned to the front line so he can be conveniently killed in battle. David needs to cover up his affair with Uriah's wife Bathsheba, who is carrying David's child.

That one maneuver cost David dearly—the child dies after a week, despite David's prayers, and David would have to deal with political unrest for the remainder of his days.

When David is old and dying, he tries to hand the throne over to his chosen successor, Solomon, the second child he had with Bathsheba. This sets off a coup attempt by another of David's sons, Adonijah, Solomon's older half brother, which makes him rightful heir to the throne. Adonijah tries to take what is his, and only serious political maneuvering and plotting by David eventually pushes Adonijah out the door and puts Solomon in his place. After David's death, Adonijah gives it another shot, and, in what is a truly unfortunate political mess, is killed by Solomon's general Benaiah.

After things settle down, Solomon finally reigns in peace. Among other things, he builds the temple, since God had said explicitly (in the same prophecy of Nathan we saw above) that David would have *nothing* to do with it—that was Solomon's job alone.

The writer of 1 Chronicles ignores all these unpleasantries and shapes a tidy and painless version of David's career. He leaves out the whole Bathsheba thing and all the political intrigue in the transition of power to Solomon that the other storyteller is so interested in dwelling on. No fight for the throne. David simply hands Solomon the crown: "Here you go, son."

This storyteller also adds—better, *creates*—a very long section, eight chapters, giving David a major role in building the temple, which, plain and simple, contradicts the previous story. Well, okay, he doesn't actually "build" the temple, but he does line everything up for Solomon beforehand, like getting the temple organized and doing a fund-raiser to make sure the temple is made of top-notch material.

Solomon may have done the actual building of the temple, but David did all the heavy lifting and passed it off to Solomon—like a controlling, fretful father lining up job interviews, securing a car loan, and finding an apartment for his college graduate son so he can "be on his own."

These two portraits of David and Solomon aren't "basically the same" with some minor details shifted around. They tell two irreconcilably different stories of Israel's founding kings. Why? Each writer was speaking to *his* time.

The writer of Samuel/Kings doesn't hesitate to highlight the political mess and personal foibles of even so central a character as David. For him, the kings of Israel and Judah are deeply flawed. He tells the story of all the northern and southern kings, and he finds something very bad to say about nearly every single one of them.

Bad leadership is for this writer *the* reason why the nation of Israel split into competing northern and southern kingdoms and both had populations carried off into captivity. His story explains why they ended up as captives in a foreign land: God is just and they deserved it.

The writer of Chronicles shapes an entirely different story of Israel's past, and trying to make the two stories fit like matching socks is impossible—one is a white knee-high tube sock and the other an argyle. Kings who have major issues in the older story practically become models of virtue and holiness—and his sanitized David is the most important example.

This new and improved David serves this storyteller's present purpose. He wants to encourage and inspire his readers to keep the faith, so he gives them a vision of the future, of what might one day be again as they await God's next move.

Let me put that another way. David and Solomon of 1 and 2 Chronicles are a *blueprint for the future,* where a king would arise to lead them again to political independence, free of foibles, with no internal political resistance. And this writer's drawn-out section on David and the temple wasn't filler or artistic flourish. It was a pep talk so his people would remember the central importance of their own rebuilt temple and their coming king's responsibility to make sure it is cared for.

Think of these stories as sermons—Samuel/Kings is more of a downer, with Chronicles casting a vision for the future. Both storytellers shape history to get their point across.

*   *   *

Seeing these two different versions of Israel's story side by side can take some getting used to. If college students wrote history papers taking liberties like this, they'd get an F and have to redo it. If publishers put out books like this on the life of Lincoln or the Civil War South, they wouldn't stay in business. We are modern people and we don't like it when someone twists and shapes the past to make a point.

Yet, here is our Bible doing just that. In plain sight, the Bible holds side by side vastly different takes on Israel's past.

The biblical historians were historians in an ancient sense of the word. We ask, "What really happened? Let's get the facts straight." I ask myself the same question—and in fact we took that path in chapter 2 talking about the conquest of Canaan. But this is not an *ancient* approach to recalling the past.

Fretting over how the Bible presents the past, which is so unlike our way, and then smoothing over the differences to make the Bible behave, betrays a deeply held, likely unconscious, false expectation that the Bible *should* act according to our alien expectations.

Cramming the stories of Israel into a modern mold of history writing not only makes the Bible look like utter nonsense; it also obscures what the Bible models for us about our own spiritual journey.

On that journey, what matters most is not simply where we've been—the triumphs or the tragedies—but where we are with God now in the moment. All great spiritual leaders will tell us that living in the moment is key to vibrant communion with God. The now is where God's presence is found, where neither past memories nor the future with its idle speculations dominates.

We are "products" of our past, no doubt, but not forever so, as if our past has written our life script in cement. We *choose*—as did writers of the Gospels and of the stories of Israel—how to read the past, what we *wish* to accept now; we adapt and transform the past into who we are and what we wish to become in our relationship with God.

The past informs the present, but it also serves the present. When the present serves the past, we are stuck in nostalgia, longing for the good old days—a sure recipe for emotional and spiritual dysfunction.

These diverse stories of the past that we find in the Bible are not a problem to be solved. They model for us the spiritual immediacy of the present.

The stories of Jesus and of Israel's dismal slide from kingship to exile also serve another purpose: they are windows onto how the Bible as a whole handles the past.

Wherever biblical writers talk about the past, we should *expect* them to be shaping the past as well.

The more comfortable we are with this idea, the better off we will be when we turn to one of the more controversial portions of the Bible when it comes to history—Israel's stories of the deep past, its origins long, long ago.

A Warm-Up for the Main Event

THE RATHER DISMAL STORY of Israel's kings that eventually ended in the crisis of exile might come across as a bit tedious and repetitive, whether you are reading the earlier version or the later version in Chronicles. All those names sound the same. Jehoiakim and Jehoiachin? Seriously? And two kings named Jehoash *and* Jehoahaz? Were these names trending or were their mothers not trying? And most every king winds up making exactly the same mistake (worshipping false gods) with predictable results (God becomes angry).

But don't let any of that fool you. The plight of Israel's kings is *the heart and center of Israel's story.*

Why would I say that? I have my reasons, and here they are.

Of the thirty-nine books in the Old Testament, thirty-four of them deal with Israel's storyline—the narrative from creation (first chapter of Genesis) to the return from exile. (The other five—Job, Psalms, Proverbs, Ecclesiastes, Song of Songs—deal with things that don't contribute to the storyline, so I'm not counting them here.)

Twenty-seven of those thirty-four books deal with the period of the monarchy, exile, and the return—and since you insist, I will tell you what those books are (according to the order in the Christian Bible): Ruth (ends with a genealogy of David), 1 and 2 Samuel, 1 and 2 Kings, 1 and 2 Chronicles, Ezra and Nehemiah (return of the exiles from Babylon), Esther (an episode of a Jewish woman in the Persian empire in the fifth century BCE), all sixteen prophetic books (the earliest deals with the events leading to the fall of the north in the eighth century BCE), and Lamentations (a lament for the fall of Jerusalem in 586 BCE).

Math nerd alert: 27 of 34 (= 80 percent) of all the narrative Old Testament books deal with some aspects of Israel's monarchy and its aftermath; or if you will, 67 percent of all the narrative chapters in the Old Testament. "A lot" for the math challenged among us. Any way you count it, this is significant.

The other seven of the thirty-four narrative books are the first seven books of the Old Testament: the Pentateuch (a.k.a. Books of Moses, Torah: Genesis, Exodus, Leviticus, Numbers, and Deuteronomy) followed by Joshua and Judges. These books contain some of the best-known stories of the Bible: creation, the flood, father Abraham, the exodus, Mount Sinai, the conquest of Canaan, and the judges (like mighty Samson).

These first seven books are Israel's stories of their deep past, or "origins stories" as they are sometimes called.

They don't exist for entertainment or for idle curiosities about the past (and definitely not as fodder for children's Bible lessons). They explain how things came to be, why things are the way they are, and most important, *how Israel got to be Israel—a kingdom with a land of its own.*

The first seven books, in other words, start in primordial time and bring us to the doorstep of the other twenty-seven, a warm-up for the main event: the kingdom of Israel.

To catch my drift, consider how often Israel's origins stories bring up the future Promised Land—the land of Canaan.

No sooner do we meet Abraham, early in Genesis, than we hear God telling him about this great patch of real estate he is going to give Abraham's descendants one day. God later brings the Israelites out of Egypt, not to let them run free, but to bring them to the very same land promised to Abraham. Then on Mount Sinai, God gives the Israelites commands—

not random feel-good commands, but instructions on how to live with one another and worship God once they got to the Promised Land. This closes out the Pentateuch.

In the book of Judges, God fights alongside the Israelites to exterminate the Canaanites in order to seize the land promised to Abraham long ago. In the book of Judges, we are in the initial, chaotic stages of settling the Promised Land. Israel's long journey, beginning with the promise to Abraham, is only completed when a king is enthroned in a national capital. Israel is born.

Israel's origins stories are an extended introduction to the meat of the Old Testament, the story of Israel as a nation with a land all its own.

Let's throw another ball in the air. The period of the monarchy is not only the meat of the Old Testament narrative of Israel. It's also the period when Israel's grand narrative *was written*.

Biblical scholars have several hundred years of some very tedious scholarly reasons for coming to this conclusion, involving a lot of Hebrew, 3-D glasses, secret handshakes, and midnight meetings. To go through all that here would put most normal people to sleep faster than Olympic trial synchronized swimming semifinals, which would keep us from getting to the point of all this.

But even from a commonsensical point of view, when would the Israelites be more likely to write down the story of "This is who we are"? As a loose association of families and tribes wandering in the desert, jotting down notes along the way? Probably not. They would be more likely to write their story after they had settled down in the land, had a chance to catch their breath, and reflect—which is to say, after they had a story worth telling and a "national consciousness" for wanting to tell it.

Israel's story, with its focus on kingship ending in the crisis of exile, probably would not have been composed until Israel was . . . well . . . a nation that had already faced crisis.

The Israelites likely wrote their story in stages over several hundred years. That process began when they settled down in the land, and especially not long after the time of David. And it got a big boost when Israel's national story went from bad to worse, from dismal to hopeless.

The first crisis, as mentioned earlier, was the Assyrian capture of the northern kingdom, with its capital Samaria, in 722 BCE. The second crisis was the Babylonian exile (586–539 BCE), when God fully turned his back on the remaining "Chosen People." He let their temple be destroyed, took their land away from them, and let them be carried off to a foreign land.

Don't think of this as a simple relocation. The southern kingdom of Judah was in *crisis.*

Losing the land and the temple meant losing God's presence. For all intents and purposes, Israel ceased to exist. Most of the prophets, including the biggies—Jeremiah, Ezekiel, and most of Isaiah—deal with this period specifically.

There's nothing like crisis to motivate you to tell your story. When you're in personal crisis (if you've never been, check your pulse), sooner or later you want to tell your story. Maybe you journal, see a therapist, get on the phone to a friend, or go to a support group.

Crisis drives us to take stock and remember who we are, where we've been, and where we hope to go. We tell our story to make sense of it all and see where to go from here.

Early on, when the Israelites were first starting out as a nation, they became more conscious of themselves as a nation and began telling their story. At the end, when all seemed to come crashing down, they *had* to tell their story, their *whole* story, from the deep past, from the beginning. And they shaped that past to help them work through their present.

One more ball to juggle, but let's sum up the first two: (1) Israel's dismal story of the monarchy is the *meat of the Old Testament,* and the origins stories are an introduction to that main story. (2) Israel's origins stories, like the stories of the monarchy, were *written during the period of the monarchy and the exile* when the Israelites were ready to write it.

Now, the third ball to keep in the air: (3) Israel's stories of kings and exile are also the *most historically verifiable* of all the Old Testament books. Let me explain what I mean and then tell you why you should care.

Even though Samuel/Kings and Chronicles spin Israel's past differently, they still clearly deal with concrete, verifiable moments of the past. We know this because—three cheers for archaeology—the biblical stories of Israel's monarchy match up well with historical records produced from other nations like Assyria, Babylon, and Persia. (For those of you who want to know more, see the reading suggestions at the end that deal with history and archaeology.)

Samuel/Kings connects well with history because the writer lived during or not terribly long after Israel's monarchy. The episodes were fresh in people's minds and they had to be dealt with. That storyteller even used official royal records of some kind with perfectly bureaucratic-sounding names like, "the Book of the Annals of the Kings of Israel." The writer of Chronicles mentions these and other sources, too. He also used Samuel/Kings as a base to work from, though, as we've seen, he adjusted it as he saw fit.

Israel's stories of the monarchy were written near the events themselves and feel more like "normal" history, with accounts of kings and battles, much of which is verified by archaeological data.

But once we go back to Israel's origins stories—before the monarchy, and especially the further back we go in Israel's story, to Israel's origins—archaeology is either strangely silent, vague, or, too often for comfort, incompatible (as we saw in the last chapter with the conquest of Canaan).

The origins stories are less connected to past history because the writers lived centuries later. They weren't reflecting on recent events still playing in people's memories. They were working with ancient tales, perhaps existing only orally, that now needed to be molded and woven together to tell Israel's *whole* story.

So, here's the point of all this, and I know it took a while to get here but we needed to do this right: if Israel's storytellers took the *recent* past, like the stories of David and Solomon, and shaped them creatively to speak to the *present,* we can bet good money they shaped the *distant* past with the same creative and *present* mind-set.

Israel's origins stories are rich and deserve to be looked at from many different angles. But we're going to take one angle that doesn't come up that much in everyday circles and that illustrates how the present shapes the telling of the past. And once you see it, you wonder how you could have missed it.

As you read Israel's origins stories, especially in Genesis, you'll notice embedded into them *previews of coming attractions,* a deliberate setup for what is to come in Israel's life later on in the Promised Land. The more familiar you are with Israel's *national* story (monarchy and after), the more you'll think, *My, this looks familiar* when you read Israel's *origins* stories.

Let me put this another way: the stories of the deep past (Israel's origins) were written to echo intentionally the present (the period of kingship ending in crisis). In a manner of speaking, that present is the deeper story being told.

A Sneak Peek at the Political Map

HOW IS THE "PRESENT" of the biblical writers seen in the origins stories? For one thing, Israel's entire national political map is already laid out in the origins stories, beginning in Genesis.

As we saw in chapter 2, the Canaanites are introduced already in the Noah story and then later in the Abraham story—an accursed, good-for-nothing brood of sinners. Israel's later hostilities toward the original inhabitants of the land are placed into ancient time to justify Israel's evaluation of the Canaanites.

The Babylonians, who razed the temple and took the Judahites captive in 586 BCE, also pop up in the early chapters of Genesis—twice.

The Tower of Babel story is about the earth's population gathered in Shinar—that is, Babylon—all speaking one language. They get it in their heads to build a ziggurat, a well-known ancient pyramid-like structure for worship with steps leading up into the heavens. For their arrogance in thinking they could approach the heavens, God comes down and confuses their language and scatters them across the earth.

Way to go, Babylonians. Way to cause confusion among the peoples of the earth. Nice one.

This story sets up the Babylonians, those who took captive the southern kingdom, as bad guys from the very beginning—the same treatment the Canaanites get in the flood story.

The Babylonians also appear in the very first chapter of the Bible, though under the radar a bit. In the late nineteenth century, archaeologists found a Babylonian story (known to us as *Enuma Elish*) that included a section on the creation of the cosmos—and it looked similar to the creation story in Genesis chapter one. For example, "water" represents chaos that is "defeated" by being split in two; a barrier overhead holds back the chaotic waters of heaven above; humanity is created last as the crowning achievement.

Babylonian culture is far older than Israelite culture, and so it seems that the Israelites modeled their creation story along the lines of the Babylonian story, not to copy it but to do it one better. Israel's creation story was its declaration—perhaps even written while under the thumb of the Babylonians in exile—that its God is superior to all the gods of Babylon, because he is the *true* creator. The Babylonians and their gods are put in their place. (We'll come back to *Enuma Elish* a bit later.)

That takes care of the Canaanites and Babylonians. Next we come to Israel's neighbors to the east, the Moabites and Ammonites. We read about their origin in the story of Sodom and Gomorrah in Genesis. Lot, Abraham's nephew, is living in Sodom, and when the angelic visitors come to destroy the town for its wickedness, they make sure to get Lot and his family out first, as they had promised Abraham.

But afterward, Lot settles down to live in a cave with his two daughters, who proceed to get him drunk so they can get impregnated. Each daughter bears him a son, Moab to the younger daughter and Ammon to the elder.

So, going out on a limb here, I'm going to say that this story doesn't exactly compliment Israel's eastern neighbors. Battles, border disputes, and other unpleasantries would later mark their relationship as nations, and those later tensions find their way into the deep past.

Next is Edom, Israel's other eastern neighbor, which finds its way into

Israel's origins story as Esau, Jacob's elder brother. Jacob was Abraham's grandson and would be renamed "Israel." Esau, who is the ancestor of the Edomites, is described as sort of a wild mountain man, a hunter, who is so stupid he sells his birthright as firstborn to his younger brother Jacob/Israel for a hot meal. My, Edom . . . uh, I mean . . . Esau is a dolt.

But Esau is also Jacob's fraternal twin, which previews the specific kind of relationship the two nations of Edom and Israel will later have: David ruled over Edom (the Edomites are called David's "servants"), though he never rules over Moab and Ammon. Later the Edomites rebel against Solomon and gain their independence, which is previewed in Genesis when Esau is told by his father Isaac, "You shall serve your brother; but when you break loose, you shall break his yoke from your neck."

To sum up, Israel's later political realities find their way into the origins story. Israel's supporting cast of characters (which also includes others we won't get into here, such as the Ishmaelites, Philistines, and Arameans) is being introduced *and already evaluated.*

That tells us a lot about what these stories were meant to do—explain the present.

And, of course, *the* central point on Israel's political map is Israel itself, whose later life is previewed as early as the story of Abraham. We first meet Abraham as he *enters Canaan from Babylon.* The Israelites will later repeat that same journey when they come home after the Babylonian exile.

Also, no sooner do Abraham and Sarah settle in Canaan than *famine* hits and they are forced to *leave for Egypt* in order to survive. While in Egypt, *plagues* fall upon Pharaoh (for taking Sarah as a wife, which is completely Abraham's fault, seeing that he passed her off as his sister to save his own neck—and who said the Bible is for kids?). Pharaoh *summons* Abraham and orders him to get out and gives him all sorts of *riches* to sweeten the deal.

Abraham's trek to Egypt and back home again mirrors Israel's exodus story. Father Jacob/Israel moves to Egypt with his sons because of a *famine.*

After a period of enslavement, *plagues* fall on the Egyptians, and the Israelites are delivered. Like Abraham, Moses is *summoned* to Pharaoh's presence, told to get out, and departs with a *nice haul of silver, gold, and clothing*.

God also makes an "everlasting" covenant with Abraham (signified by circumcision)—a solemn agreement to stick by him no matter what. God would later make an everlasting covenant with David, too. Connecting David to an ancient figure like Abraham would show great honor to David and give his kingship more street cred for those who needed convincing.

The overlap between Israel's ancestors and the political realities of the monarchy is not a coincidence. Genesis previews what's ahead, the meat of the Old Testament—Israel's life in the land.

And the brilliant writer/editor of the Pentateuch makes the same point from yet another angle.

Playing Favorites
with Little Brother

ALL THROUGH ISRAEL'S ORIGINS STORIES, God has this unexpected habit of favoring younger brothers over their elder brothers. In ancient cultures, including Israel, and most cultures that have appeared on this planet, firstborn sons have status: they are next in line to be king, inherit the wealth, get Dad's truck, sleep in the biggest bedroom, have their college paid for, etc. But Israel's story goes against the grain.

Already early in Genesis, God favors the sacrifice of Abel the younger over the sacrifice of his older brother Cain. The story doesn't clarify exactly why Abel was favored; readers are left hanging. We read, though, that Cain kills Abel out of anger. So why this story? Why here? It's not clear, until we keep reading and see the pattern, embedded here, that runs through Genesis—and throughout Israel's entire story: the younger is mysteriously favored over the elder sibling.

Abraham's elder son Ishmael is pushed aside in favor of second-born Isaac—because God commanded it. The birthright and blessing of Isaac's elder son Esau winds up falling into the hands of the younger son Jacob, who will soon be renamed "Israel" and will father twelve sons, the fountainheads of the nation's twelve tribes.

Joseph, of Amazing Technicolor Dreamcoat fame, is the youngest of

Jacob's eleven sons, yet he winds up ruling over his elder brothers as Pharaoh's right-hand man in Egypt. Next comes Moses: God's chosen one to deliver Israel from Egypt is the younger brother to Aaron, Moses's right-hand man.

The younger brother leapfrogging over the elder brother pattern is all over the place in the stories of Israel's deep past. By the time you get to Israel's national story, the pattern is thrown right in your face and won't go away.

King David—Goliath slayer and greatest of all of Israel's kings—is the youngest of his brothers and the least likely to be Israel's king, yet he is God's unexpected choice. Israel's next king, David's son Solomon, is . . . wait for it . . . not the firstborn, as the next-in-line-to-be-king rules dictate. Yet he too is God's choice over Solomon's elder half brother Adonijah to sit on the throne in Jerusalem.

Then, after the nation of Israel splits into northern and southern kingdoms, the one to survive, the one to return from exile and reclaim the land, is the southern kingdom, the "younger" of the two.

This is huge.

The southern kingdom was made up of the tribes of Judah and Benjamin. Their ancestors, according to the book of Genesis, were not the firstborn of Jacob/Israel's sons. Judah (after whom the southern kingdom was named) was the fourth son of Jacob and his first wife, Leah. Benjamin was the son of Jacob's beloved wife Rachel, and youngest of all twelve of Jacob's sons.

Israel split into north and south because of serious political tensions between them. And after they split, they battled each other in war for decades. In the stories in Genesis, the brothers don't get along very well, either: Cain kills Abel, Ishmael is left to die in the desert, Esau wants to kill Jacob, Joseph's brothers throw him down a well and then sell him into slavery.

The nation of Israel is "sibling rivalry" on a national scale.

Let's throw into the mix the fact that the southern kingdom, the one that came out on top—*compiled and composed Israel's story in the wake of the crisis of exile.*

Stories of sibling rivalry in Israel's deep past, where the younger comes out on top, don't just "happen" to look like the story of the divided kingdom. The "younger brother," the southern nation of Judah, scripted their long drama and eventual triumph into the stories of Israel's deep past.

Israel's origins stories, with God's preferential treatment of the younger sibling, were written to explain why the southern kingdom, the "younger brother," survived Babylonian exile whereas the elder (and larger and more powerful) northern "brother" was wiped off the pages of history by the Assyrians 150 years earlier.

Whatever history there is (in the modern sense of the word) in Israel's origins stories is a matter of debate among scholars—like did the Israelites actually begin as an extended family from father Abraham?—but we don't need to get into all the details here. My point is that Israel's stories of the deep past were not written to "talk about what happened back then." They were written to explain what is. The past is shaped to speak to the present.

Israel's story of the *deepest* past—one of the most familiar stories in the entire Bible—is also shaped to explain the present.

Adam, Who Art Thou?

A FIRST COUPLE named Adam and Eve, a forbidden piece of fruit from a forbidden tree, a talking serpent, and a whole lot of trouble. Those moments in the story that begins the Bible are familiar to many. What doesn't get nearly as much airtime, however, is how this story, like other stories in Genesis, previews Israel's later life.

Actually, the story of Adam previews Israel's entire story from beginning to end.

Many just assume that Adam was the first human in the Bible, but humanity was already created by God earlier, on the sixth day of creation, according to the very first chapter of Genesis. Now we meet Adam in the second chapter of Genesis, whom God formed out of the "dust of the earth," as the story puts it.

If humans were already created in chapter one, this Adam guy God created in chapter two doesn't seem to be the first human. So who is he? Adam is Israel's whole story told in two chapters, Genesis 2–3.

As the story goes, Adam is created by God out of dust and then placed in the lush plot of land, the Garden of Eden, God's dwelling place. Since this is God's property, God makes the rules. He gives Adam one clear command: "Eat anything you want, Adam. Knock yourself out. But *don't eat of the tree of the knowledge of good and evil.*"

The arrangement is simple. If Adam obeys, he will dwell in paradise.

If he disobeys, he will die "that very day." Adam and Eve wind up breaking the command by eating the fruit of the forbidden tree—yet they don't die that day, at least not physically. The story tells us, rather, that they are driven out of the Garden—*exiled*—barred from God's land by armed angels standing guard at the entrance.

Obey and you stay; disobey and be exiled. Israel's story follows the same pattern.

After God delivers the Israelites from the humiliation of Egyptian slavery (created out of dust, so to speak), he places Israel in a lush land, Canaan, a land flowing with "milk and honey." As with Adam, God makes the rules: he gives Israel commands to follow, the law given to Moses on Mount Sinai. If the Israelites obeys those laws, they will live long in the land and enjoy God's blessing. If they disobey, they will be tossed out of Canaan, exiled to a foreign land.

Again: obey and you stay; disobey and be exiled.

The Adam story plays on the idea that exile is a kind of "death"—a spiritual death, separation from God's presence. That's why "on the very day" that Adam eats from forbidden fruit he doesn't actually die, but he *is* driven out of the Garden.

Elsewhere the Old Testament describes the land of Canaan as the place of "life"—God is present and brings blessings on his people. Exile to Babylon, however, is "death"—away from God's presence in the land, to the place of curses, of punishment. The prophet Ezekiel sums it up nicely in a creepy vision of a valley filled with dry bones that slowly grow muscles and veins and come to life. That may read like a script for *Zombie Mega-Apocalypse 3,* but it's a vivid symbol of the Israelites "dead" in exile coming back to life when they reenter the land.

The story of Adam, from life with God to death in exile, is an abbreviated version of Israel's story. Rabbis have noticed this since at least the medieval period, and for good reason.

Oh, and have I mentioned that the Book of Genesis tells us "Israel" in Hebrew means "struggle with God"? No? Well, I just did. Israel's long epic of *struggling* to obey the commands of God during the period of the monarchy, and the loss of the Israelites' homeland that resulted, is scripted into the dawn of time by Israel's storytellers.

The Adam story, then, is not simply about the past. It's about Israel's present brought into the past—even as far past as the beginning of the human drama itself.

But Israel's storytellers will put Israel's story even further back than that.

The Exodus *Story*

EXODUS. You've probably seen the movie, which still hits TV screens every Easter. A burning bush, "Let my people go," water turns to blood, people die left and right, Charlton Heston breaks up with Anne Baxter so he can marry Herman Munster's wife (Yvonne De Carlo), the Red Sea parts down the middle, slaves are delivered from Yul Brynner's evil clutches, laws are carved onto stone tablets, Edward G. Robinson undermines the whole thing. It's a classic.

The movie is four hours long, but consider the topic. We're at a key moment in Israel's deep past, perhaps *the* key moment. Israel is born—out of the oppression of Egyptian slavery, poised to begin its long journey to nationhood, guided by God along the way.

As key as the exodus is, the story has taken some hard hits over the past century or so from a historical point of view—and you don't need to be a scholar to know this. Just keep an eye on PBS, *Nova,* or the History Channel, or look at most any college-level introduction to the Old Testament.

Modern historians are puzzled that no ancient source, including Egyptian ones, even hint at an event of this scope. A band of slaves, numbering about 600,000 men according to the Bible—2,000,000 people counting women and children (the population of Baltimore)—marched out of Egypt after their God drowned the Egyptian army and crippled the empire into submission. And no one mentions it?

Maybe the Egyptians left no record because they were too embarrassed to admit they were bested by slaves and their desert-dwelling God. Perhaps, although political spin was always an option. Remember King Mesha from chapter 2? "We were overrun by the Israelites because . . . uh . . . our god was angry with us. (Yeah, that'll stick.)"

And even if Egypt did keep this public embarrassment under wraps, we would expect nearby nations to have jumped all over it—again and again: "Gather 'round and let me tell you the story of the fall of mighty Egypt, how Pharaoh and his army cowered before simple slaves and their mighty god." But nothing.

Historians would also expect to find some physical trace somewhere of a massive number of Israelite slaves living in the Nile delta ("land of Goshen" as the Bible has it). But we've got nothing—at least nothing positive. In their records, Egyptians did mention "Asiatic" slave labor, but that is a generic term and doesn't mean they were Israelites.

And a massive movement of people wandering the desert for forty years should leave some trace, but, again, nothing. And it's not like no one's been looking. If archaeologists can find evidence of prehistoric hunter-gatherers, is it too much to ask to find *some* evidence—anything—of enough slaves to fill a midwestern city migrating through the desert to their new homeland 3,200 years ago?

The later stories of Israel's monarchy have no problem mentioning the names of hostile kings, like Shishak of Egypt, Mesha of Moab, Sennacherib of Assyria, Nebuchadnezzar of Babylon, Cyrus of Persia, and others. But the Pharaoh *who began Israel's four hundred years of slavery*? No idea. The book of Exodus introduces him as "a new king [who] arose over Egypt." Did the writers just forget his name? Was it an unimportant detail? Or is this another clue that we're not dealing with history on the same level as the later stories?

I feel pretty strongly, actually, that the exodus story has some historical basis; it wasn't made up out of thin air. A story of national origins that begins "we were slaves" doesn't sound like the kind of thing people would try to come up with to make an impression. Perhaps a much smaller number of "Asiatic" slaves—a few hundred or so—left Egypt under the leadership of a charismatic figure and made their way to Canaan. (And the name "Moses" looks Egyptian, like Thutmoses—King "Tut.") Over time the story was told, and retold, and re-retold over generations, reshaped over time, with its final version being the one we read in our Bible.

That's a plausible explanation among biblical scholars, but we can't say for sure. I'm happy to keep an open mind, and in the meantime I've learned to be fine with not knowing. But whatever we do, we can't make believe the historical problems of the exodus story don't exist.

As history, the exodus story has some challenges. But as a *story*—well. Watch out. It carries serious punch, which we miss if we focus on the historical angle. Through this story, Israel's storytellers were tying their people not simply back to Adam (even though that's pretty far back), but to the first moments of creation itself and the cosmic realm—to the opening chapter of the Bible, to Genesis chapter one.

When Gods Fight

WHATEVER HISTORICAL ECHO there is in the exodus story, Israel's storytellers clearly exerted a lot of effort to dress it up in unhistorical clothing.

Some call that unhistorical clothing myth, and that's a perfectly fine word—as long as we remember "myth" doesn't mean "silly things we made up while on acid."

Myths were stories that were part of ancient ways of describing ultimate reality, which is found not here and now but on a higher and more primal plane of existence, the behind-the-scenes actions of the gods in primordial time. The ripple effects of those "back then and up there" actions were believed to echo in the here and now with every sunrise, budding plant, birth, and pretty much everything else that surrounds us.

Myths, in other words, were deeply meaningful stories that connected the present world with the heavenly and eternal realm.

Myths also played a role in national origins stories. "Who we are as a people is ultimately rooted in the actions in the divine sphere long ago; we are here because of what the gods set in motion in days of old."

For example, earlier we glimpsed a Babylonian story called *Enuma Elish* (gesundheit). In this story we read of the god Marduk winning a cosmic battle at the dawn of time by slaying Tiamat. Not only is Tiamat Marduk's great-great-grandmother (talk about family dysfunction), but she is also the symbol of watery chaos.

By cutting Tiamat in half (filleting her lengthwise), Marduk made the chaos a habitable place. With half of Tiamat's carcass he made a barrier overhead to hold back the waters above, and with the other half the earth below. By slaying this watery chaos and making the habitable world, Marduk was acknowledged as the high god, the god above all the other gods.

Here comes the political angle. Marduk, who won the cosmic smack-down, just happened to be the god who also handpicked Hammurabi to be king of a new Babylonian dynasty (around 1750 BCE). Get it? Since Marduk handpicked Hammurabi's new reign over his people, to contend against Hammurabi was to contend against Marduk himself. The story of Marduk's victory justified and legitimized Hammurabi's regime. The ripple effects of this cosmic creation are seen in the creation of a nation.

The Israelites have a national founding narrative of their own rooted in the divine realm. Which brings us to the exodus story—and here is where you probably want to forget you ever saw the movie.

God sends ten plagues on Egypt and then parts the Red Sea, thus delivering the Israelites to begin their rise to nationhood. But these acts weren't a random flexing of God's muscles to intimidate Pharaoh. Exodus is a story of Israel's beginnings rooted, too, in a battle between the gods: Yahweh (God's personal name in the Old Testament) smacks the Egyptian gods upside the head to show them who's boss.

As long as the Israelites are in Egypt under Pharaoh's thumb, they are also under the control of Egypt's gods—and Pharaoh was considered one of those gods. Yahweh won't allow his chosen people to be forced to serve other gods, so he will wage war and get them back. So this God of an enslaved desert people, whom Pharaoh had never heard of, marches into the territory of the world's superpower and dominates its "powerful" gods like he's Muhammad Ali taking on a schoolyard bully.

If we miss that mythic theme of a "divine battle," we miss the drama and energy of the exodus story.

Yahweh begins toying with Egypt's gods with the very first encounter between Moses and Pharaoh. Moses throws his staff down before Pharaoh and it turns into a serpent. The cobra was a symbol of Egypt's power, which is why Pharaohs wore those funny hats that made them look like cobras (or an '80s hair band). Pharaoh's holy advisers, armed with their own divine strength, smile politely and duplicate the same feat without breaking a sweat. Moses's serpent, however, swallows the serpents of Pharaoh.

The symbolism is screaming at you: the God backing Moses is greater than the gods backing Egypt. In the first meeting between Moses and Pharaoh, we already see how this whole scene is going to go down.

Which brings us to the ten plagues. The first plague turns the Nile River and all of Egypt's water supply into blood. The Nile was the source of Egypt's existence and was worshipped as a god. A Nile turned to blood wasn't just "really weird"; it symbolized the defeat of the deity: Yahweh can turn Egypt's source of life, supposedly protected by its god, into a source of death.

The second plague makes frogs multiply all over Egypt. The Egyptian goddess of fertility, Heqet, who was supposed to have control over all that, was depicted with the head of—you guessed it—a frog.

Jumping to the ninth plague, Yahweh darkens the sun. The high god of the Egyptians and the patron god of Pharaoh is the sun god Ra (similar to how Marduk was Hammurabi's patron god). Yahweh just snaps his fingers and blots him out, which does not send a promising signal for the fate of Egypt.

On the eve of the departure from Egypt, God sends his tenth and final plague upon the Egyptians: the death of all firstborn in all the land. He announces this final blow by saying that he will execute judgment "on all the gods of Egypt." The Egyptian god of the dead is Osiris. By controlling death on Osiris's home turf, Yahweh has Osiris in a headlock and is moving in for the pin.

The plagues aren't random tricks. They are, as it turns out, a one-sided cage match featuring, in this corner, the up-and-coming challenger, Israel's God, Yahweh, and in the other corner, the reigning champions, the gods of Egypt. The bout goes ten rounds, with Yahweh the clear winner in each. In fact, in the eighth plague, Pharaoh cries uncle and is ready to let the Israelites go. But Yahweh "hardened Pharaoh's heart" so he wouldn't let them go. Yahweh isn't done with Pharaoh yet—like a cat toying with a mouse, reviving him so she can keep playing.

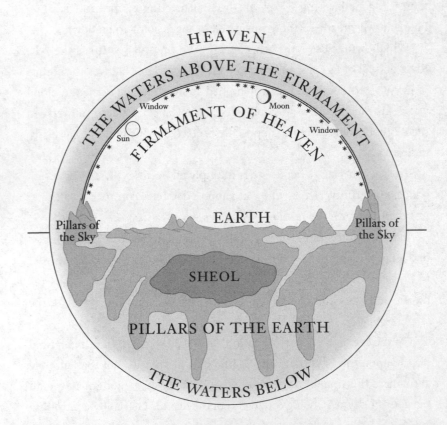

The knockout blow comes at the parting of the Red Sea. God splits the sea in two, revealing the dry ground below. The Israelites march to freedom and a *nation* is born, to be sure, but let's not miss the symbolism here. Israel's national birth story echoes the six-day story of *creation* in Genesis chapter one.

Before God begins creating, "darkness covered the face of the deep." "Deep" is the Old Testament way of referring to the primordial waters of chaos, like we see in *Enuma Elish* (where it is personified as Tiamat).

After creating light on day one, God turns his attention to the deep. On day two, God *splits the deep in two*, pushing it apart, to form waters "above the dome" and waters below. The dome produces an air pocket, so to speak, what we would call "sky" or "atmosphere."

Then on day three, God sets his sights on the waters below—a vast body of water covering the entire earth. He divides it to reveal dry land beneath, which is precisely how the parting of the Red Sea is described in the book of Exodus. By splitting waters not once but twice, God formed the sky, oceans, and land, which will later be filled with air, sea, and land creatures, including humanity.

Israel's storytellers describe their national origins (exodus), the creation of their people, in terms of warring gods and waters of chaos split in two—a "here and now" replay of the "back then and up there" creation of the cosmos. The God who tamed chaos to create the cosmos also tamed Pharaoh and his gods to create Israel.

Water figures into both stories—as it will in a third.

What's with All the Water?

THE BIBLE has one more mythically robed story involving God and water: the story of Noah and the flood. Israel's storytellers drew a clear line linking the stories of creation, Noah, and the exodus.

Like the exodus, the flood story has history behind it. Many biblical scholars relying on geological findings believe that a great deluge in Mesopotamia around 2900 BCE was the trigger for the many flood stories that circulated in the ancient world, some already two thousand years old by the time King David came on the scene.

These stories all reflect the belief that the flood was divine punishment. In a well-known Mesopotamian version of the story found in what scholars call the *Atrahasis* epic (named after its main character), the flood was divine punishment for humans making too much noise and so keeping the gods from their rest. The biblical story takes a very different approach. As over-the-top as the biblical story seems to us, the Israelites didn't place the blame at the feet of sleep-deprived grumpy gods. The fault was human wickedness and evil.

Be that as it may, my point here is that the flood story, though rooted in history, is dressed up in mythic clothes from head to toe. The flood wasn't an out-of-control rainstorm. Creation, all that God had done in Genesis chapter one, was falling back down on itself. Creation was being un-created. Order collapsed back to disorder.

The heavenly dome ("firmament" in many English Bibles) that kept the chaotic "waters above" at bay on day two of creation had "windows" (see page 122). The flood is the result of God opening these windows to let the "waters above" come crashing back. Then the "fountains of the deep" open up and the "waters below" come gushing forth. The waters separated at creation crash together from both sides, undoing creation and returning the cosmos to its original, precreation, chaotic state.

Those who are not on God's side in the days of Noah (everyone except Noah and his family) are drowned—just like the enemies of God, the Egyptians, are drowned when the divided Red Sea comes crashing back down on itself—a mini-replay of the flood.

Noah and his family are saved by an ark that God tells him to build and line with pitch, a tarlike waterproofing material. If I can lay a little Hebrew on you, the word for ark is *tevah* (TAY-vah), and it occurs in only one other place in the entire Old Testament: the story of Moses.

To escape Pharaoh's edict to kill all the male children by throwing them into the waters of the Nile, Moses's sister places him in a basket—a *tevah*—likewise waterproofed to keep it from sinking.

Just as God brings Noah safely through a watery ordeal in an ark, Moses also floats to safety on the Nile in an "ark." A bit later, all Israel will also be brought safely through a watery ordeal when they pass through the Red Sea on dry ground.

I know we're keeping a lot of issues afloat here (pun intended), and reading the Bible with an ear open to Israel's ancient way of thinking can be hard work. No doubt.

But it's worth the time.

In all three stories—creation, Noah, and the exodus—God is in full control of water: When water is held back, there is life. When released, there is destruction for God's enemies but safety and a new beginning for God's people.

Okay, why are we talking about all this? Why go into the exodus, the creation story, the flood, and dysfunctional Babylonian divine families? Because it helps us to see what Israel's storytellers were doing.

The biblical writers, we recall, worked sometime between the beginning of the monarchy to well after the return from Babylon. They rooted their origin story, their "national creation" long ago, in the stories of even longer ago, in primordial time, the time before time—the creation of the cosmos.

The creation of Israel as a people was at the hands of the same God who created the cosmos. The God who tamed the cosmic enemy, the teeming, chaotic waters of the deep, also tamed the enemies at Israel's "creation," the Egyptians and the gods that supported them.

The mighty God of old is still present with Israel. Israel's existence as God's Chosen People is scripted into primordial time and the realm of the divine.

I understand how this might take some getting used to for readers with certain expectations of the Bible—like it should avoid myth and just give us more or less history as we understand the term. But especially here in reading the stories of Israel's deep past we need to be extra careful not to allow *our* point of view to dictate how the Bible behaves.

A story like the exodus story is what happens when, as I said previously, God lets his children tell the story—in ways *they* understand and that is packed with meaning for *them*.

These are ancient stories. For ancient Israelites to talk about their God as the ultimate chaos tamer back at creation was a bold statement of faith—now none of the gods of other nations could hold that spot. And then for this God to show up and perform a smaller version of that act to get their ancestors out of Egypt—well, "that'll preach," as my Baptist friends would say. Maybe not so much today, but definitely then.

For the ancient Israelite storytellers, living in the shadow of the crisis of the divided monarchy and then the exile to Babylon, the takeaway point of all this is: we are still here, for the God of old, the mighty creator, the one before time, the God of "back then and up there" is on our side here and now.

That is a summary of Israel's faith. This is Israel's story.

Stories Work

HISTORY IS HUGE for the Christian faith. What Christians believe about God is rooted in real time and space events (even if we can't explain how), where God actually showed up somehow and did something—especially when it comes to Jesus. So when the Bible says that such and such happened, the default response is to take it at face value as *our* kind of history.

But the Bible itself complicates matters: its writers are clearly engaged in consciously shaping the past rather than simply reporting it.

The modern period of historical research also hasn't always helped the "Bible has to be our kind of history" idea. Even Israel's core moments—the exodus and conquest of Canaan—take a serious tilt toward story and away from a modern kind of history.

"Did what the Bible says happened really happen?" has been a nagging, even crippling, question for Christians for generations and is still a big reason why some people either keep away from the faith or leave it.

And that question isn't going away, which is why we needed to spend some time in this chapter looking at the question of history from different angles. (And you may have noticed this chapter is even longer than the previous one. I promise to be better from here on out! I do!)

The Bible and history is a polarizing issue. On one extreme we have those giddy with excitement that now, finally, we know the Bible is a lie and we can get over it. On the other extreme we have those who go to an all-out, full-court defense to protect the Bible from any such "attack," taking no prisoners and giving no quarter to those who say otherwise.

With those extremes, it can be tough to carve out some space to think through hard issues in peace and quiet. Thoughtful questioners are often left in a dangerous no-man's-land attracting hostile fire from both sides.

As I see it, *both* sides—the "now we know the Bible is a pack of lies" side and the "Bible has to be historically accurate to be the Word of God" side—are wrong because they start from the same wrongheaded premise: any book worthy of being called "scripture" has to, if anything, get history "right."

And just what do these sides mean by "get history right"? They mean what modern Westerners think it means: reporting facts more or less as they happened, with minimal to no spin or elaboration. Both sides start with a faulty expectation of the Bible—whether or not they say so openly, or even realize what they are doing. They've painted themselves into the same corner and have been clawing each other's eyes out for generations.

As a person of faith, journeying onward along the Christian path, I want to do my best to take the Bible for what it is. I want to try, as best as I can, to watch how the Bible behaves and then try and understand what sorts of things the Bible is prepared to deliver. I want to align my expectations with the Bible as an ancient text and accept the challenge of faith: letting go of how I think things should be and submitting to God.

There's an irony: the passionate defense of the Bible as a "history book" among the more conservative wings of Christianity, despite intentions, isn't really an act of submission to God; it is making God submit to us.

In its most extreme forms, making God look like us is what the Bible calls idolatry.

Over the years I've grown more and more convinced that "storytelling" is a better way of understanding what the Bible is doing with the past than "history writing." This conviction is both intellectual and spiritual, and that journey began for me already in seminary, when I was exposed, even in a protective sort of way, to the differences in the four Gospels and in the two stories of Israel. The study of archaeology and other matters of antiquity in my doctoral work pushed me further along.

The questions guiding me over the years have been driven by faith: "Why does God do it *this* way?" and "What does *this* Bible tell us about God?" Even if I don't have the final answer to these questions, a way forward has become clearer for me: *maybe God likes stories.*

Stories work. Stories are powerful. Stories move us deeply, more so than statistics, news reports, or textbooks. We all know that. We only need to think about what holds our attention and makes us long for more—that book, film, or TV series that we wish wouldn't end quite so soon, that story told of some deep, personal, transforming experience, whether painful or joyous.

The Bible, then, is a grand story. It meets us and then invites us to follow and join a world outside of our own, and lets us see ourselves and God differently in the process. Maybe that's really the bottom line. The biblical story meets us where we are to disarm us and change how we look at ourselves—and God.

The Bible calls that change repentance. Maybe stories are where repentance can happen best. From what I can see, I think the Bible's storytellers would agree.

*   *   *

We began this book by looking at Canaanite genocide as the main example of God's violence in the Old Testament. Handling that issue well meant getting to know something about how the writers of the Bible talked about the past: as storytellers, not as "historians" in a modern sense.

In this chapter we looked more closely at how the Bible's storytellers shaped the past. Even when writing about things that happened in relatively recent history, they had no problem adding, changing, and even overturning the past to speak to their present. One of the clearest places we see this at work is where we began this chapter: the same past events portrayed in very different ways sitting right next to each other—Israel's monarchy in the Old Testament and the Jesus story in the New.

These differing portrayals are a window for us to see how Israel's writers portrayed the past in general.

The Bible includes multiple voices when speaking of the past. Next we're going to look at multiple voices elsewhere in the Bible—and by elsewhere I mean pretty much wherever you look, even where we might expect the Bible to stay within the lines: when talking about what God is like and what it means to obey him.

Even there the Bible doesn't behave itself. And especially there, an owner's manual approach to the Bible doesn't work. At all.

Rather, God is challenging us again to venture out, leave familiar surroundings, and explore—even if that means having to climb up some high hills and down some deep canyons.

Why Doesn't God
Make Up His Mind?

Raising Kids by the Book
(FYI, It Doesn't Work)

Daughter, age ten, to father (sobbing): Daddy (*sniff*), I'm sorry I broke your favorite mug (*sniff*). I know how much you like it. I'm such a klutz (*sniff, sniff*).

Father to daughter: Hey, it's only a mug. Don't you worry about it. You didn't cut yourself, did you?

Son, age thirteen, to father (indignantly): Wait a minute. I broke your stupid staple gun last week and you made me pay for it.

Father to son: Your sister is having a rough time thinking she is dumb and clumsy, and she means more to me than a mug. You, on the other hand, have a habit of abusing my tools—such as last week's gem where you used my staple gun to hammer nails. It's time for you to learn some responsibility.

Father to mother concerning son, age three: HE'S GOT A KNIFE IN HIS HANDS!! GET IT!! GET IT!! HURRY!! BEFORE HE IMPALES HIMSELF!!

Father to son, age twelve: Hand me that circular saw, but be careful. Make sure it's unplugged and the cover is over the blade.

Father to son, age twenty-five: Chain's dull. You'll want to replace it with a nice, new, sharp one before you cut down that oak.

> *Father to daughter, age eight:* Okay, you can have *one* cup of soda, but
> no more.
> *Father to daughter, age fourteen:* Okay, but just *one* sip of my wine.
> *Father to daughter, age twenty-one:* I recommend the White Russian,
> but tell the barkeeper not to be skimpy on the vodka.

*   *   *

They never told us—the nurses, I mean, the ones who sent us home with our first child, with no plan, no adult supervision, not even a brochure on how to raise these things. They just shipped us off with a "romantic dinner for two" (a.k.a. last meal ever), two T-shirts sporting the hospital logo, a fruit basket, a baby cap knitted by elderly volunteers, and a hearty pat on the back.

I can still see them smirking as we left—that knowing smirk. I didn't get it then. Now I do. I hate them so much.

Stop me if you've heard this one, but parenting is hard, unpredictable, and no script is available to guarantee results. Guidance and advice abound, but at the end of the day it's just you and your offspring—no net, no sure sense you're moving in the right direction and that things will turn out just fine if you stick to the plan.

Being "consistent" with your children day after day and year after year, and treating each child and each situation "the same" sounds nice on paper, and I'm sure you mean well, but in real life it flops more than the Brazilian soccer team in the penalty area. Life happens, children mature differently, and each situation is unique. Life mocks our puny attempts to nail down a sure set of parenting rules.

Parenting is winging it, and each time you do, you learn more so you can learn to wing it better and better. There. That's all the parenting advice you need. Now would be as good a time as any to collect any parenting books you might have, tie them in a bundle, and leave them on the curb.

Likewise, spiritual maturity won't happen by looking to the Bible as a one-size-fits-all-how-to-grow-up-Christian instructional manual. We can't "go to the Bible" for ironed-out answers, or even principles, to many—or most—of the specific and important decisions we make every second of the day, on the fly.

Waiting for the Bible to "tell me what to do" means we'll either be waiting forever, in silence, paralyzed about making any decisions, or we'll wind up baptizing our bad decisions with a Bible verse that, let's face it, has about as much to do with what we're dealing with at the moment as a Shakespearean sonnet has for guiding roof repair.

Rather, as we'll see, different parts of the Bible appeal to us at different times and on different points in our walk with God. It's all good, but not as a quick and ready answer key to life—find the verse and voilà, smooth sailing.

The Bible itself makes this quite clear by being so utterly disinterested in giving straight answers to questions we'd think really should have straight answers.

Like God, for instance.

Looking to the Bible to find out what God is like seems like the most obvious thing the Bible should hand you on a silver platter. But it doesn't. You have to work for it.

The God we meet there sometimes knows everything, and other times he's stumped and trying to figure things out. He's either set in his ways and in full control of the situation or he changes his mind when pressed. He gives one law in one place and then elsewhere lays down another law that requires something else. Sometimes he's overflowing with compassion and at other times he has a hair-trigger temper.

You'd think the Bible wouldn't make the God question harder than applying for a home equity line of credit (which inexplicably took me four months, by the way, and I'm having trouble letting that go). If God is behind the Bible, why doesn't he just get to it in a five-point summary, or perhaps a white paper with clear answers to everything we need to know so we're not left scratching our heads and so theologians don't have to debate for centuries and write fifteen-hundred-page books on "the nature of God"? If the Bible isn't clear even about big issues like God (!!), what's it good for?

Maybe the real problem here, once again, isn't the Bible but expecting from the Bible something it's not set up to do. Maybe the Bible isn't God's owner's manual for us that answers all our questions about God and lays a script out for us to follow as we walk along the Christian path.

The Bible, as we've already seen, is a *story*—a story of God's people on their long, diverse, up-and-down, spiritual journey; a story written by different people, under different circumstances, for different reasons, spanning more than a thousand years. It was written during times of peace and war, in safety and exile, in Israel's youth and chastened adulthood. Its writers were priests, scribes, and kings, separated by time, and geography, not to mention Myers-Briggs personality types.

A book like that isn't going to be a consistent one-size-fits-all instructional manual that *tells* us—in all our varied circumstances—how to grow into a life of faith.

A book like that *shows* us what a life of faith looks like.

As all good stories do, the Bible shapes and molds us by drawing us into its world and inviting us to connect on many different levels, wherever we are on our journey, and to see ourselves better by its light by stirring our spiritual imagination to walk closer with God.

That's how the Bible acts as a guide for the faithful—by being a story, not by giving us a list of directions disguised as a story.

When we try to squish the Bible's diverse voices into one voice, we are no longer reading the Bible we have—we are distorting it and cutting ourselves off from what it has to offer us. The Bible *shows us* how normal and expected it is for all people of faith to be a part of the same sort of process, the same spiritual journey, of living, reflecting, changing, growing in our understanding of God, ourselves, the world, and our place in it.

If there's a sense in which the Bible "tells us what to do," I think that's it: as a model of the diverse and unscripted spiritual life, not as our step-by-step instructional guide.

"If I Wanted to Tell You What to Do, I Would Have"
—God

FOR A FIVE-SECOND tour to see how the Bible doesn't work as an owner's manual for life, we only need to flip to the book of Proverbs, Israel's book of ancient wisdom sayings.

Toward the end of the book, we find two proverbs sitting there right next to each other. Both are wise sayings, but they give the exact opposite bit of advice. They're trying to act all innocent and inconspicuous, but don't let them fool you.

> 1. Proverbs 26:4: *Do not answer fools according to their folly, or you will be a fool yourself.*
> 2. Proverbs 26:5: *Answer fools according to their folly, or they will be wise in their own eyes.*

In other words, (#1) Don't mix it up with argumentative morons, or you'll come down to their level. On the other hand, (#2) Get in the face of argumentative morons to put them in their place.

Looking to the Bible for a detailed road map for life might leave one feeling a bit light-headed right now. Which is it? Which one do I do? Stop jerking me around, Bible! JUST TELL ME!

No chance. Proverbs doesn't tell its readers what to do, because Proverbs teaches *wisdom*.

Wisdom isn't about finding a quick answer key to life—like turning to the index, finding your problem, and turning to the right page so it all works out. Wisdom is about *learning how* to work through the unpredictable, uncontrollable messiness of life so you can figure things out on your own in real time.

Both of these proverbs are good, wise, and right—the question is *when* each is good, wise, and right. And that "when" depends on the situation you might find yourself in.

Sometimes you need to walk away from the know-it-all at the office party, and other times you need to expose someone's ignorance at a staff meeting. Which you choose to do depends on a list of factors like: What sort of relationship do you two have? Do you two have any history? Is your coworker under some stress that is influencing her actions right now? What sort of feedback—if any—is more likely to help at this moment for all involved?

You get the point. What needs to be done at that moment can't be scripted beforehand. In real life, you have to wait until the moment is upon you and then do what you think is best right here, right now, in this situation, with this person.

Wisdom, like what we see in the book of Proverbs, doesn't tell you what to do. It shapes you over time so when the time comes when you have to think on your feet, you can make a wise decision. Wisdom makes you fit to think for yourself when you need it.

When my son was ten years old, he asked if he could watch *Saving Private Ryan*. It's certainly the best war movie I've ever seen, and the first few minutes (invasion of Normandy) is a graphic and sobering reminder of the horrors of war.

All my son's friends had seen it, and he wanted to see it, too. I could

have said, "If all your friends jumped off a bridge, would you do it, too?"
That's the standard state-issued parent comeback we are required to use at
least twice yearly—and sometimes it's the right response, but not always.
I decided to watch it with him, to let him join his peers. I judged him to
be ready for it, and it turned out to be a wise move.

I did not let my daughters watch it, not because they were girls, but
because they were eight and five at the time. Knowing them as I did, I
judged they were too young and did not need a powerful and emotive
movie like this to be placed in front of them. They had not reached that
point of maturity. The "when" was right for my son, but not for my daughters. And even when they turned ten, that would not automatically mean
they follow their brother's lead, since not all ten-year-olds have the same
emotional constitution (or interests).

So far so good, but not long after this scene we got together with Christian friends of ours who had a different approach to parenting. I made
sure to announce—mainly because I am a troublemaker—that I let my
son watch *Saving Private Ryan*. The mother gave me one of those "you're
a complete idiot" looks and blurted out, in an attempt to checkmate my
dumb parenting move, "Proverbs 22:6."

I said (now in Socratic mode), "What's that?"

She said (quoting the Proverb), "Train children in the right way, and
when old, they will not stray."

I said, "OK. And?"

She said, "It's an R movie. Children should never watch R movies.
You're not training them in the right way."

I said, "I don't see that in Proverbs 22:6. And what exactly is wrong
with R movies? Are they all the same?"

We went on like this for a while. This mother, well intentioned and
loving as she was, was treating Proverbs like a detailed script for all life,
each step plotted out. I was treating it as a rough map with broad outlines
that I had to fill in as best as I could at the moment.

In my mind, I actually *was* "following" Proverbs 22:6 by *letting* my son watch *Saving Private Ryan* and by *not letting* my daughters watch it. This proverb isn't one-size-fits-all. None of them are. Proverbs actually give surprisingly little actual information about what to do. We need to fill in the details and decide when, where, with whom, and how a particular proverb works.

The book of Proverbs contains a few hundred of these sayings, and it never works like an owner's manual.

Say you have an issue with money and you want to know what God thinks, so you turn to the book of Proverbs. You find out soon enough that Proverbs has a lot to say on the subject—and no two proverbs fully agree.

One proverb says, *The wealth of the rich is their fortress; the poverty of the poor is their ruin.* This sounds simple enough. Wealth is a fortress with walls—it protects you. Poverty ruins you. If you don't believe it, see what happens when your credit score dips.

But then we come to another proverb. It begins in a similar way, *The wealth of the rich is their strong city,* but it ends differently, changing direction 180 degrees: *in their imagination it is like a high wall.* Living in a "strong city" (a "fortress") isn't protection as it was before. Now, it can make you cocky, thinking your wall is so high nothing can get in.

In other words, watch yourself. Wealth can protect you from ruin, but it can also bring you to ruin through pride.

Another proverb takes it a step further: *The wage of the righteous leads to life; the gain of the wicked to sin.* Now it looks like having and not having are neutral; whether wages benefit you depends on the kind of person you are, "righteous" (a just and fair person) or "wicked" (not just and fair).

A fourth proverb takes yet another angle: *Those who trust in their riches will wither, but the righteous will flourish like green leaves.* Riches aren't something to depend on at all, but being "righteous" is.

So what does Proverbs say about wealth? Different things. But what does God want me to *do*? Wrong question.

Each proverb is true depending on the situation and it's up to us to figure it out. The first proverb might work for a hardworking person. Greedy TV preachers and large Wall Street banks that use taxpayer money to bail themselves out of the mess they created need to hear numbers two, three, and four. It all depends.

Now, here's where all this talk about Proverbs is headed: *think of Proverbs as a snapshot of how the Bible as a whole works.*

Treating Proverbs—or the Bible—as an ironclad, fixed-in-cement rulebook isn't an option. We need to think for ourselves and figure out what to do with what we read. Maybe we shouldn't expect the Bible to hand us answers to life to be checked off one by one.

When Biblical Writers Get Cranky

PROVERBS may not connect the dots of our lives, but it's clear about one thing: *eventually* you can count on God.

Following the path of wisdom, with discipline and perseverance, *will* bring you to a good place in due time. The journey may not be easy, and probably won't be, but it's worth the effort. As one proverb says, "The teaching of the wise is a fountain of life."

If only the Bible stopped right there—but it doesn't.

Turn to the very next book and you come to Ecclesiastes, which has issues with this "be patient, it will eventually work out" vibe.

The main character of this book, named Qohelet, is at the end of his rope. He's seen enough in his life and thinks wisdom is one big fat waste of time and effort. He drops bombs like, "For in much wisdom is much vexation, and those who increase knowledge increase sorrow," and later, "Do not act too righteous, and do not act too wise; why should you destroy yourself?"

He sounds upset. Maybe he hasn't read Proverbs yet. Or maybe he has and it's not working for him.

Proverbs and Ecclesiastes, sitting side by side as they are in our Bible (the Christian Bible, at least), are a beacon fire on a hill, telling us in no uncertain terms that the Bible is not an instructional manual for the Christian life, but something to be wrestled with.

Qohelet is the most pessimistic person in the entire Bible. You can't count on God, he says, and wisdom makes no practical difference, because at the end of the day we all die anyway.

For Qohelet, death, in a word, sucks. Death is permanent, life is temporary, so death ultimately wins. Seeking wisdom to live better, as Proverbs says, is a cruel divine joke.

And don't try telling Qohelet that everything will work out in the afterlife—he's not convinced there is one. He's never seen it and neither has anyone else. All we know is that we die, and, to add insult to injury, after you die you will be quickly forgotten just like you've already forgotten those who died before you.

Not the most uplifting message you'll find in the Bible, especially the last part, but the guy's got a point. Watch the Oscars where they pause to remember the members of the Screen Actors Guild who have died since the previous year. Note how many have slipped by you—"Oh yeah, she *did* die, that's right." You're struck by the names, remember fondly, but as soon as you change the channel or check Facebook, you've already forgotten.

The dead escape our minds. We forget so quickly—even some of our own loved ones. We eventually can go days and longer without calling to mind a departed grandparent or even a parent. Soon we find ourselves having trouble remembering what year they died—maybe even your grandparents' names take a few seconds to come to mind.

And when's the last time you called to mind your great-grandparents, and great-great-grandparents—by name—and blessed God for them?

And we haven't even gotten to the bazillions of people who have died throughout human history whom we've never heard of, not to mention the countless people alive today who will one day die and whose names and faces will be forever unknown to 99.9999 percent of the rest of us.

Real ball of laughs, this Qohelet. Thanks for the reminder. Is he *trying* to ruin our day? I think he is.

And what's most depressing for Qohelet is that God—get this—actually set up the world to be like this, so it's all God's fault. "So you'll excuse me," says Qohelet, "if I can't be bothered with wisdom: there's no payoff." Today we'd call this an existential faith crisis.

Unlike how our friends at church might respond to all this, neither Ecclesiastes nor any other book of the Bible tries to solve Qohelet's dilemma or correct him for being a rebellious, faithless heretic: "There, there, Qohelet. You've had a bad day. Now get over it and buck up. God's not like that at all. Maybe you just need a good nap. Have you tried reading your Bible every morning and having quality prayer time?"

The book just leaves it all out there, respecting the struggle. The only positive nudge is in the last few lines of the book (which many scholars think was added later on by an editor): to paraphrase, "Life is hard, isn't it? It sure is. Keep going anyway."

Here's the point: the Bible, a book that tells us about God, has right next to each other two books that have such *different takes on God.*

Proverbs puts us on the path toward gaining true wisdom for all that life throws at us. After reading Proverbs you're supposed to say, "I've got a lot to learn, but I can do this. God's wisdom is guiding me. I'm learning more every day, and I'll get there, eventually."

Qohelet is angry with God and pretty much dares him to show up and make a miserable world right. But at the end, the miserable world stays as is and Qohelet doesn't come to a happily-ever-after conclusion. After reading Ecclesiastes you're left with, "Everyone dies, life is absurd, God is to blame, and I don't like him very much. Not sure I can keep taking one step after another on this journey—but I'm going to try to keep moving anyway." Qohelet is in despair, his "dark night of the soul" as the medieval Christian mystics put it.

These books don't agree, and that's fine, because they are not two chapters in God's big book of rules to live by. Both are *portraits* of God and the life of faith, and both are in the Bible. And both are valid.

Both are there waiting for us when we need them, as we plod through our own messy journey of faith. If you're questioning God, are about to give up, and need to rant, Qohelet is your guy. If that's not your issue, but you're on a path to try to live your life wisely, Proverbs has a lot to say.

And either way, God is with you.

"Rulebook Bible reading" shortchanges the depth and raw reality of Israel's own journey of faith in God. Both Proverbs and Ecclesiastes belong in the Bible just as they are, because both situations are real experiences for those on the same journey.

And then there's Job.

"Don't Quote the Bible at Me, Please. I'm God."

–God, to Job and His Friends

JOB HAD A GOOD LIFE—for a while. He lived obediently before God, was a husband and father of ten, and had livestock and riches like no one else. After family get-togethers, Job would offer some sacrifices to God just on the off chance his children may have sinned. If anyone is doing it right, it's Job.

So what does God do? Give Job a pat on the back? Of course not. He allows a member of his heavenly court (more below), a being referred to only as the "Adversary" (more below), to make Job miserable.

This "Adversary" claims that the only reason Job is righteous and just is because God has made it too easy for him, blessed with family and riches and all that. In other words, Job worships God because of what is in it for him.

The Adversary bets God that if he were to take away all his stuff, Job would be found out for the superficial God worshipper he is. God takes the bet and tells the Adversary to have at it, only he needs to spare Job's life.

Soon Job's livestock are stolen or killed along with his servants; a wind blows a house down on top of his children, killing them all; and Job is smitten with painful sores from head to toe. All of this prompts Job, understandably, to curse the day he passed through his mother's birth canal. He also wonders what in the world God is doing to him.

Enter Job's three friends. They mean well. First they sit down by his side for seven days and nights without saying a word, tearing their robes and heaping ashes on their heads as a sign of mourning with their good friend, who is such a mess they hardly recognize him.

After seven days, the three friends (later in the book joined by a fourth) begin to talk to Job, which leads to a very long series of speeches where they each take turns trying to make Job feel even worse. They are bent on "helping" Job see that he *must* have done something to deserve all this, and if he repents of his sin, God will alleviate his suffering. After all, God doesn't just punish for nothing.

Job, however, will have none of it. He insists all the while that he is innocent. He has done nothing wrong and he can't figure out why God is making him suffer so.

Of course readers of the book of Job know all about the bet, even though Job and his friends don't, so we know Job really is innocent, and after a few pages his friends start to get a bit redundant and annoying with their accusations. They just can't let go of the idea that Job deserves what he's getting, and the fact that Job keeps defending himself is part of the problem: he is proud and needs to repent, get right with God, so his life can get back to normal.

Don't be too hard on Job's friends. They're not mean, insensitive, or unreasonable for harping on the "you must have done something to deserve it" idea. That idea comes straight from the Bible.

Actions have consequences. Adam and Eve are kicked out of the Garden of Eden because they disobeyed God. Israelites are given Torah. If they obey, they will be blessed; if they disobey, they will be cursed. (Take a glance at Deuteronomy 27–28 to see this idea in action.) And the whole reason the Israelites were taken into exile was because of disobedience.

Then you have the book of Proverbs, which is all about "actions have consequences." Living a wise, obedient life leads to God's blessings; living a foolish life of disobedience leads to God's curses.

Put yourself in the place of Job's friends who took seriously this biblical view of God as someone who treats people according to their actions. They pay their friend Job a visit and see he is clearly suffering some consequences. They draw the reasonable biblical conclusion that Job must have done something to incur God's wrath.

Job's friends diagnose Job's condition by the book. They were well within their right, according to the Bible, to lean on Job and get him to admit what he had done wrong.

This back-and-forth goes on for most of the book until God shows up at the end. Apparently God doesn't think much of these long-winded speeches, for mortals don't know enough to know what God is up to. After all, God says for four whole chapters, "I'm the creator, you're not, so let's start by you all keeping your mouths shut rather than thinking you have the right to question me."

I think most readers of the book might be looking for a little more compassion from God at this point—or maybe he could have let Job and his friends in on the bet he made with the Adversary. But God opts for another approach: "I am God, shrouded in mystery, and you need to learn how to deal with that."

Then as he concludes his speech, God says this to one of Job's friends: "My wrath is kindled against you and your two friends; for *you have spoken to me what is not right,* as my servant Job has." So after all the "don't question me" business, God tells us all who have been rooting for Job what we've been waiting to hear: Job was right and his friends were wrong.

Job's friends. They were fine people, I'm sure, and they were technically right if you're going by the book. But God says they are wrong.

So it seems like God isn't operating by the book. The book doesn't limit God. There is more to God than what the book says. God is bigger than the Bible.

Proverbs, Ecclesiastes, and Job all agree: the Bible doesn't capture a freeze-frame of God and bind him to it. If we get on board with this idea, some other things the Bible says about God will make more sense.

Is There More Than One God?
(And, No, This Isn't a Trick Question)

YOU'D THINK THE ANSWER to this question would be a no-brainer. *Obviously* there's only one God in the Bible. Any other "gods" are make-believe. What kind of a dumb, lame question is that, anyway?

Actually, it's a great question that stares us in the face when we pick up the Bible and start reading it.

In the ancient world, gods were more common than smiling politicians in an election year. Each nation had its fair share. These gods were worshipped in the form of idols—statues created of wood or stone that made the gods "present" to the people.

In some places, the Old Testament describes these other gods and their idols as no gods at all, more of a joke than anything. The prophets Isaiah and Jeremiah ask sarcastically how gods made out of stone and wood could really be gods, seeing that wood and stone are, well, wood and stone. Israel's God, Yahweh, was the real God, the creator, and thus too real to be captured in anything created by human hands. And he gave the Israelites strict instructions not even to try—the Second Commandment tells them not to make any "images" of Yahweh.

In one famous story, the prophet Elijah challenges the priests of Baal—the high Canaanite god—to a duel: whichever god can make fire come from heaven and consume the sacrifice on the altar is the real deal. The priests of Baal cry and plead with their god to make it happen, but he is as dead as his stone idols.

After mocking the priests about how their god must be taking a nap or something, Elijah steps up to the plate, and, to rub it in, has his altar doused with water. After a prayer, fire flashes down from on high and the sacrifice is burned to a crisp.

Game, set, match. There is no God but Israel's God, and it's plain stupid to think otherwise.

So far so good, but that's only part of the biblical story.

At least as often, the Bible treats these gods as *real,* actually existing, and who have to be reckoned with. Israel's God isn't the *only* God; he's the best and mightiest *among the gods.* All of Israel's neighbors had a high god, sort of a chairman of the board over the lesser gods. For Israel, Yahweh was this high God. It's right there in the Bible, in black and white.

Back to the book of Job. There we saw a heavenly meeting, a gathering of the lesser gods come to present themselves before Yahweh in what looks like a weekly staff meeting.

The Adversary is one of those divine beings, the one who challenges Yahweh's high opinion of Job. In English Bibles this divine being is often called Satan, but don't think of that as a personal name of someone in red tights and holding a pitchfork. *Satan* in Hebrew simply means "adversary." This divine being in Job isn't king of the underworld but a member of the heavenly board playing the role of prosecuting attorney (which is why some English translations call him "the Accuser"). Yahweh gives this divine being free rein to make Job the singularly most miserable person in the entire Bible.

Some of the psalms operate with the same notion of a divine board meeting. In Psalm 82, Israel's God takes his place in the heavenly CEO chair and pressures the other gods. Apparently, the kings these gods are supposed to keep tabs on are not acting justly, and God holds the gods responsible.

Other psalms say things like, "Yahweh is a great God; a great king *above all gods*," and "Yahweh is great; our Lord is *above all the gods*." The other gods exist, but when compared to Yahweh, they don't hold a candle. In fact, the comparison only makes sense if the other gods are believed to exist.

What makes Israel's God better than the other gods?

For one thing, he is the true creator of the cosmos. In the stories of Israel's ancient neighbors, creation is a group activity and involves, as we've seen, some sort of conflict among the gods—as in the Babylonian story *Enuma Elish,* where Marduk slices Tiamat in half to make the sky and the earth.

In the biblical creation story, however, we see no conflict, no battle. Israel's God acts alone and speaks things into existence.

But even in the biblical creation story, God says, "Let *us* make humanity in *our* own image." Who is "us"? Does God have a mouse in his pocket? (Please say no.) Even though we see no conflict between the gods, "us" still refers to the other divine beings, lesser gods, as we see in Psalms and Job.

God seems to consult this "divine council" (as it is often called), though, unlike the other stories, these gods don't do anything. They sit there and watch the high God go to work. Israel's God is the "great God above all gods." He is the creator, and no other gods—and certainly not the gods of other nations.

Yahweh also deserves high god status for another key reason. He delivered the Israelites from slavery in Egypt.

As we saw in the last chapter, the plagues are a ten-round, lopsided battle pitting Yahweh against the gods of Egypt, with the crushing blow coming at the Red Sea, where God once again controls the waters of chaos as he did at creation.

At this point you might be asking—and probably should be—"Wait a minute. Are you saying there actually *are* dozens of other gods running around?" No, I don't for one minute think there are heavenly board meetings or battles among the gods.

But I believe the Israelites believed these things. And that's my point.

They lived in a world where the existence of *many* gods was a given, like church steeples piercing the skyline in towns across America. They confessed Yahweh's greatness the only way they could in that culture, the only way that would have ever dawned on them: in contrast to the gods of the other nations.

Israel's story doesn't lay down at every point what all the faithful for all time *should believe* about God. It *shows* us how Israelites understood God on *their* journey with God, in their time and place.

Think of it this way. When a young child is convinced there are monsters in her closet, that's all there is to it. Her father can either say, "Ah, grow up. There *aren't* any such things!! (Dumb kid.) Let me open the closet door and show you nothing's in there but clothes and toys." That would be factually true, but of zero help to the frightened child.

By contrast, a father—one who passed his how-not-to-be-an-idiot-father test—would meet his daughter where she is conceptually and say, "Let me take a look."

He'd open the closet door and close it behind him. He'd make a racket by knocking around some hangers and boxes and come out with an unbuttoned shirt, his hair messed up a bit, claiming victory. "I crushed them. They were crying and whining like babies. One of them looked at me and wet himself and ran away. They *won't* be coming back. Now you can sleep safely."

Likewise, God's voice to the Israelites in the Old Testament meets them where they are. God allows himself to be talked about, worshipped, and trusted by the Israelites within the boundaries of that ancient horizon.

"How many gods exist?" seems like a pretty basic question for the Bible to get right, but even here the Bible doesn't speak with one voice. The answer to that question depends on what parts you are reading—just like the question about money in Proverbs, or about God in Proverbs or Ecclesiastes.

The Bible reflects diverse views of God because the Bible records Israel's diverse spiritual journey.

At some point later on in their journey (we don't know exactly when), the Israelites settled on a final answer to the question: only one God exists. For both Jews and Christians today, that one answer remains true, and the other biblical portrait of God—where he is one among many—is left behind.

The portrait of God that the ancient Israelites assumed for much of their history—that he is the best God among the many—is not factually true. And, I have to believe, God is fine with us drawing that conclusion.

Leaving some of the Bible behind is only a problem when the Bible is seen as an A–Z sourcebook of timeless information. It's not a problem when the Bible is seen as a model for our own walk with God, where who we are and where we are affects how we understand and connect with God.

God Seems Like a Regular Joe

A FRIEND OF MINE once asked me how I visualized God right now, at this moment. He's a real pain with these probing sorts of questions, so, naturally, I told him to mind his own business, and then gave him some academic babble about how God is a being that can't be pictured, is beyond our comprehension, blah, blah. As all my good friends do, he ignored me and kept interrogating.

I gave in after a while and came to see, lo and behold, that I actually did have a mental picture of God—and I hesitate to tell you what it is. I imagined God somewhere off in the distance, like he was tucked away in a corner of the ceiling veiled behind a dark cloud. At least that was my picture at the time.

I've passed that story on to others over the years and realized I'm not alone. And we can't be held fully responsible. Portions of the Bible paint a similar picture of God—a far-off sovereign, a king seated high on his throne, inaccessible, who looks down from on high.

In the creation story in the first chapter of Genesis, for example, God is on high, above it all looking down, totally in control. He makes the heavens and the earth in six days through a series of commands ("Let there be light," etc.) and puts everything in its place, including the sun, moon, and stars, without breaking a sweat, like he's moving chess pieces on a cosmic board. Other parts of the Bible present God in similar ways, a deity who is above the fray and has to be called upon to make a cameo appearance.

Another portrait of God in the Bible, at least as common, usually doesn't come to mind as quickly when we talk about God: God is more "one of us." He figures things out, changes his mind, regrets his own actions, reacts to what others do, and has to be calmed down.

Once again, we see two very different portraits of God in the Bible.

This more "human" God appears on the world stage immediately after the six-day creation story. He forms Adam out of dust, like a hands-on potter, not on high giving a command as before. After forming Adam, God sees he is alone, and so, thinking on his feet, he tries to rectify the situation. He makes the animals and parades them in front of Adam to see if one of them will do as a suitable companion, but, alas, not one does. God seems to be making it up as he goes along.

He moves to plan B and puts Adam under the knife to create a woman from his side. When he wakes, Adam says, "This *at last* is bone of my bones and flesh of my flesh." At last. Finally. Creating animals to ease Adam's loneliness didn't work, but forming a being like him did.

After Adam and Eve eat the forbidden fruit, they hide because they are ashamed of their nakedness. God, who is taking a human-like stroll in the Garden of Eden at the time, notices they are missing but doesn't know where they are, so he calls out, "Where are you?" God then punishes these humans and banishes them from the garden. Clearly things are not going according to plan. God is caught off guard. Another plan B.

God in the Adam story doesn't act like God in the first chapter in Genesis, the high above-it-all God where everything is ordered and executed perfectly according to plan.

Flip ahead a few pages and we come to the story of the flood and Noah's ark. God sees how sinful humans have become and seems caught off guard again. He is "sorry" he ever started this project and is greatly "grieved" about it. Things are not proceeding as he had planned and he reacts—some would say overreacts—in fury: he wipes out every single living creature with a massive flood, keeping eight humans and two of each animal behind to start over.

A few pages later we come to the story of Abraham, Israel's first ancestor. God gives old Abraham and old, barren Sarah a son, Isaac. Then God tells Abraham to offer him as a sacrifice, that is, take him out and slit his throat.

So why does God command Abraham to kill the miracle baby? The story is very clear about that: God is *testing* Abraham to find out whether he "fears" him.

So Abraham (with a lot less hesitation than you might expect) takes Isaac up to Mount Moriah and ties him to an altar loaded with kindling. Just as he is about to bring the knife down onto his son, God intervenes through an angel, saying, "Do not lay your hand on the boy or do anything to him; for now I know that you fear God. . . ."

Now I know. God found something out he didn't know before. Abraham fears God. He has passed the test.

One more example, this from the book of Exodus. After the Israelites cross the Red Sea and arrive at the foot of Mount Sinai, Moses climbs up the mountain to meet with God. While there, the Israelites below, who were apparently in need of some serious adult supervision, build a calf out of gold—an idol, a way of making God present with them. After all, Moses is up there having God all to himself, and everybody else in the world has idols to keep their gods nice and close. So Aaron, Moses's brother, builds them one. What's the harm?

The harm is that the second of the Ten Commandments says, clear as a bell: "You shall not make for yourself an idol." When Moses comes back down and sees the golden calf and the New Orleans Mardi Gras surrounding it, he smashes the tablets with the laws written on them. After hearing Aaron's lame excuse ("but . . . but . . . they made me do it"), Moses agrees to go back up the mountain to see what he can work out with God, who is surely displeased.

More than displeased. As in the flood story, God is absolutely fit to be tied. He has had enough and decides to give up on the whole plan. God informs Moses that he will turn his back on the very people he rescued from Egypt: an angel will lead the people, but he will keep his distance. Otherwise he would consume (kill by fire) the Israelites along the way. God isn't sure he can control himself.

So Moses reasons with God—and he gets him to *change his mind* back again to the original plan. Moses reminds God that the Israelites are his people, and all the other nations know it. If he just walked out on them, what would everyone think? How would they ever learn that the Israelites are special and their God is the true one?

Moses plays on God's sense of honor and shame to convince him not to give in to his anger—and it works.

Seeing God as a character in the story who can be talked to, reasoned with, shows regret, finds things out, and changes his mind can be troubling because it doesn't sound very much like the sovereign signal-caller of the universe.

What kind of God takes advice from puny humans and then calms down? What kind of God needs to be calmed down in the first place? What kind of God regrets what he's done? What kind of God needs to test his subjects so he can be sure of their loyalty?

Why does the Bible have to make this so complicated? Why can't the Bible have God act like God, everywhere?

But this ungodlike God of the Bible gets at the very heart of both Jewish and Christian beliefs about God. This God doesn't keep his distance but embraces human experience and becomes part of the human story. He is "on the scene" with bracing regularity.

In the Christian story, God steps further down. He becomes one of us, God in the flesh.

We actually need God to be less of an on-high-keeping-his-distance kind of God, and more a God who reacts, changes his mind, and can be reasoned with.

Without a God like that, the whole idea of prayer can't get off the ground. Think about it: "Oh Lord, *I'm begging you*, please . . . ," and fill in the blank—healing from sickness, comfort in suffering, a new job, the Stanley Cup finals. Many prayers are about thanking and praising God, and sometimes a prayer can be silent contemplation.

But prayers are often cries of help designed to *convince* God to see things our way.

Jesus himself pleaded with God. The night before Jesus was crucified, we read in Luke's Gospel, Jesus prays so hard to get out of being executed that he sweats drops of blood. Jesus is determined to go through with it, but he still asks God if there is a way out. Jesus knows the plan but tries to see if God would change it.

This "present" God of the Bible, who is with his people and not off at a distance, is the same kind of God we need on our own spiritual journeys.

God certainly is a multidimensional character in the Bible. Sometimes he is up there and out of the way, unmoved and unmovable. But more often he is the kind of God you can actually have a relationship with. Both are in the Bible. Neither cancels the other out, but—ironically, perhaps— the biblical God that is least Godlike is the one we tend to connect with more in our day-to-day lives.

A God like us is not a problem. The New Testament, where God becomes one of us, calls this Good News.

God Lays Down the Law
. . . Sort Of

ANOTHER PLACE where we might expect to see consistency in the Bible is with the laws God himself gave the Israelites to follow. After all, we're talking about the law that God inscribed on stone with his own finger and hand-delivered to Moses on Mount Sinai.

Plus, for any laws to work, let alone God's, they have to be consistent. "Red means stop, usually" won't work. And for the Israelites, keeping God's laws was more serious than obeying traffic laws. Breaking the law had consequences, including the death penalty in some cases, banishment, or a national disaster like being exiled to Babylon.

But rather than lining up to eliminate any confusion, Israel's laws don't behave as we might expect them to. Here are some examples, and I'm including chapter and verse to make it easier to look them up quickly. According to the Bible, these laws are all revealed by God to the Israelites on Mount Sinai.

Can Israelites keep their fellow Israelites as slaves?

Exodus 21:2–11: Yes, and the males can choose freedom after six years.

Deuteronomy 15:12–18: Yes, but both male and female slaves have the option of freedom.

Leviticus 25:39–43: No way, no how, are Israelites ever to be
enslaved to each other. Remember, you were once slaves in Egypt.
Hire them as laborers, but don't make them slaves. That's what
foreigners are for.

Can Israelites eat the carcasses of mauled animals?

Exodus 22:31 and Deuteronomy 14:21: No. You're holy and that's
disgusting.

Leviticus 11:39–40 and 17:15: Sure, but you'll be "unclean" till evening. Make sure to wash your clothes.

Can a man have sex with a woman during her period?

Leviticus 15:24: Okay, but if you do, you and every bed you lie on
will be "unclean" for seven days.

Leviticus 20:18: Absolutely not and no seven-day time-out, either.
You and the woman will be "cut off" (perhaps death or excom-
munication), because this sort of thing is no different than having
sex with your sister or aunt.

Where exactly are we allowed to offer sacrifices to God?

Deuteronomy 12:13–14 and Leviticus 17:1–8: Only in one place, in
God's sanctuary. Don't even think about sacrificing anywhere
else.

Exodus 20:24–26: Wherever you want. Knock yourselves out. You
can build an altar of earth, but if you want to use stones, make
sure they aren't carved with a knife. Also, don't have steps going
up to the altar, lest your nakedness be exposed.

How do we celebrate properly the Passover meal?

Exodus 12:8–9 and 46: Make sure you roast the Passover lamb (and
whatever you do, definitely do *not* boil it or eat it raw) and eat it at
home.

Deuteronomy 16:7–8: Boil the lamb and eat it only in the central
  sanctuary.

These are just a few examples, but they are enough to make the point:
Israel's laws sometimes contradict each other.

We're not the first ones to notice. The ancient Israelites were already
aware. For example, our old friend the writer of Chronicles saw the contradictory Passover laws and offered a solution. Writing generations after
the Israelites returned from Babylonian exile, he *merged* the laws of Exodus
and Deuteronomy (2 Chronicles 35:13): the Israelites are to *roast* (= Exodus)
the lamb and *boil* (= Deuteronomy) other meats. Problem solved.

Which raises a perfectly sane question: Why are the laws given by
the same God to his people so different? Welcome to the world of careful
Bible reading. Jewish scholars have pored over these laws since before
the Christian era to try to figure them out—as in the early example from
Chronicles that I just mentioned.

Over the last several hundred years, biblical scholars have proposed
theories to explain why these contradictory laws exist in the same book.
One explanation has gotten the most traction—actually, almost universal
traction: Israel had more than one "legal tradition."

These traditions (or "law codes" as they are sometimes called) were produced independently by—stop me if you've heard me say this already—
different groups of Israelites, living at different times and in different
places, and each reflects different ways of understanding what God's will
is for them.

The editors of the Bible, who lived after the return from Babylonian
exile, compiled these law codes in the way we see them in the Bible today.
And when you bring these diverse traditions together to produce one long
version, you're bound to have the kinds of tensions and contradictions we
see in the examples above.

Different law codes existing within the same Bible is similar to what
we discussed in the last chapter, with the four versions of Jesus's life and

the two versions of Israel's monarchy. Of course, when you have *separate books* sitting side by side—like the Gospels and the stories of Israel—the differences are more obvious. The editor(s) of Israel's laws, however, didn't hand us separate versions of the laws. Instead the various laws were woven together into one story, the story of Moses receiving God's laws on Mount Sinai and delivering them to the Israelites below.

The differences can be harder to see, but they are there—and they tell an important story for readers of the Bible today.

The editors of the Bible were obviously quite happy to include these law codes just as they are and leave them be. They didn't smooth things over, and they didn't seem to fret over how confused this would make God sound to people like us. The Bible they were happy to produce is complicated, challenging, and messy—and if you believe God had some say in producing the Bible, you have to conclude that God was apparently quite happy to let them do it.

So if even Israel's law book—the part of the Bible you would expect to work as a "rulebook"—resists a "follow the script" attitude, what then does that tell us about the Bible as a whole?

Probably that it doesn't work as a rulebook, either.

Even when the Bible talks about God, the laws that God wrote down and gave to Moses, or just generally what God expects from us, the Bible speaks with more than one voice. That's only a problem if we bring to the Bible our own false expectations.

The Bible is not a Christian owner's manual but a story—a diverse story of God and how his people have connected with him over the centuries, in changing circumstances and situations.

That kind of Bible works, because that is our story, too. The Bible "partners" with us (so to speak), modeling for us our walk with God in discovering greater depth and maturity on our journey of faith, not by telling us what to do at each step, but by showing us a journey of hills and valleys, straight lanes and difficult curves, of new discoveries and insights, of movement and change—with God by our side every step of the way.

*   *   *

New discoveries, movement, change. We will continue to hear this same tune as we turn now to that part of the Bible Christians call the New Testament—only there the tune gets a bit louder, even deafening in places.

According to the Gospel writers and Paul, the story of Jesus was too radical, too new, too unexpected to fit fully into former ways of thinking about God and what it meant to be the people of God.

These early followers of Jesus, most of whom were Jewish, certainly respected and revered Israel's story; they believed that the Jesus story was deeply connected to it, and that the same God who had been at work previously was at work in their own time.

But they also saw that God was pushing them beyond the boundaries of Israel's story, because Israel's story wasn't set up to handle the unexpected story of Jesus—of a messiah who was executed by the Romans and then came back to life.

So these writers transformed Israel's story, rethought it, changed it, adapted it, and in some cases left parts of it behind to describe this unforeseen move of Israel's God.

When it comes to understanding the Bible, these first Christian writers have something to say to Christians today, and it's this: getting the Bible right and getting Jesus right are not the same thing.

Thinking they are runs the risk of missing the point of what these writers were trying to say.

Jesus Is Bigger Than the Bible

Jesus Gets a Big Fat "F" in Bible

I TEACH BIBLE COURSES to college students, and I absolutely love it—mainly because I have complete and unquestioned control over their puny lives and they fear me with a great fear.

They fear me because I grade their work, and if you've never had the thrill of grading undergraduate papers in Bible, please find some way to do so, especially if you like marking things with a red pen. Red pens, as we all know, are the industry standard for telling students they are wrong, and with that comment we loop back to my opening point about controlling students' lives.

Anyway, my lawyers and dean are even now advising me to get to my point and avoid further self-incrimination.

As college Bible students learn soon enough, the Bible is not an easy book to get your arms around, at least once you start paying attention to the details and dig in. Some do very well. Others not as well but they are in the ballpark and I'm proud of them.

But now and then students come up with rather bizarre readings of the Bible that look more like free association than a college paper, and I am driven to despair, wondering what I did wrong and how I can keep this quiet.

To avoid libel charges, here is a hypothetical example. In Genesis 31 Jacob is fleeing his father-in-law Laban's house with some items that belong to Laban. Verse 22 says, "*On the third day* Laban was told that Jacob had *fled.*" So Laban and his men go after Jacob to get his stuff back, and they catch up to Jacob seven days later.

What if a student were to interpret verse 22 to mean that Jesus rose from the dead *on the third day* and *fled* from the grave?

Exactly. I would dip his paper in a bucket of red ink, give him an "F" for the assignment, and make him endure some sort of in-class shaming ritual that college admissions officers never bother to mention on campus visits.

Upon further advice from my lawyer and my dean: "I'm kidding about the shaming part, and my intention was never to imply anything derogatory about anyone, real or imagined, and I apologize if my words were taken that way."

But my main point holds. Loosey-goosey handling of the Bible gets you a bad grade, because you can't just make the Bible mean whatever you feel like making it mean. You have to stick with what the text says. Everyone who takes the Bible seriously knows that.

Except for Jesus.

In the Gospels, Jesus quotes and interprets his Bible in ways that might make some Bible readers today very uncomfortable.

One example comes from Luke's Gospel. Jesus finds himself in a debate with the Sadducees, a Jewish religious party that was in charge of the temple.

Unlike most other Jews, Sadducees thought the idea of people rising from the dead was nonsense. In this story they try to stump Jesus by posing a hypothetical scenario: if a woman is widowed and marries her husband's brother, and he dies and she marries another brother, and it happens four more times (seven husbands in all), which brother would be her husband at the resurrection?

Jesus responds that marriage is a nonissue at the resurrection, because they will be "like angels." Fair enough, but to make his point stick, Jesus quotes from the book of Exodus.

In the story of the burning bush, God appears to Moses and announces who he is: "I am the God of your father, the God of Abraham, the God of Isaac, and the God of Jacob." Jesus quotes this verse as biblical proof that God "is not the God of the dead, but of the living, for to him all are alive."

It's okay to be confused.

No one reading this episode in the book of Exodus would ever think for one second that resurrection is the topic. It's simply a story of Moses meeting God for the first time and God introducing himself as the God of Israel's long-dead ancestors. Now Moses knows whom he's dealing with.

No reasonable connection exists between what the burning bush story says and what Jesus says it says. Jesus is engaging in a bit of creative biblical interpretation. Specifically, Jesus is exploiting the *present* tense verb "I *am*," meaning that God is, *right now as Jesus is talking,* the God of an *alive*—resurrected—Abraham, Isaac, and Jacob.

Again, it's okay to be confused.

Watching Jesus handle his Bible can be a head scratcher. If I got this sort of thing from a student, I'd call it free association and the red ink would pour from a fire hose.

But I don't think I'm really in a place to grade Jesus: I want to understand him.

Jesus didn't read his Bible the way we today might expect him to. He wasn't bound by the words on the page of his Bible and what they meant. Two factors explain why Jesus handled his Bible the way he did.

First, Jesus was Jewish. The example above, however strange it might look to us, fits right in to the creative approach to handling the Bible that Jesus shared with his fellow Jews. And so to understand how Jesus read his Bible we must, once again, leave our expectations at the door and see Jesus—yes, even Jesus—as a man who was a full-fledged member of the ancient Jewish world.

Second, as we'll see more clearly below, Jesus often read his Bible in fresh ways that challenged old ways of thinking about God and what it means to be the people of God. Specifically he often focused attention on himself, as if he was somehow not simply interpreting the Bible but that he was the Bible's focus. Jesus did that enough to attract a lot of negative attention from Jewish teachers and other authorities of Judaism.

Taken together, when it came to reading his Bible, here's the bottom line about Jesus: he didn't stay inside the lines the way many Christian readers today assume the Son of God would. Jesus, of all people, did not feel bound to follow strictly what the Bible said. Jesus was no rulebook reader of the Bible. Jesus was bigger than the Bible.

Jesus Was Actually Jewish
(Go Figure)

WHATEVER WE MIGHT THINK of how Jesus read the burning bush story, Luke tells us what the crowd thought of it: "Then some of the scribes answered, 'Teacher, you have spoken well.' For they no longer dared to ask him any more questions."

They loved it, and that's our hint: Jesus was not the first or only Jew to give Bible reading a creative twist. His handling of the Bible fit into the Jewish world at the time.

Like any Jew of his day, Jesus *revered* his Bible (especially Torah). He also understood, along with his contemporaries, that *creative* readings of the Bible (that look like free association to us) are completely in step with that reverence.

Revering the Bible and handling it *creatively* might sound like a contradiction to us, but it wasn't to ancient Jews. To understand why, and therefore to understand Jesus, we need to back up for just a second.

As we saw in chapter 3, the Old Testament (more or less as we know it today) was produced by the Israelites in the generations after they returned from the exile in Babylon (539 BCE). These writings—some of which were being produced at that time and others that were much older and now gathered together—told the Israelites' ancient story and eventually became an authoritative guiding document for their present life and future hopes.

In other words, these writings *came to be* revered as sacred scripture, Judaism's main connection with the mighty acts of God of old, a timeless memorial to the past as they lived their lives in the present.

The big problem the Jews faced, though, was that their scripture was set in writing while the world around them kept changing.

They no longer lived in the bygone days of the monarchy when Torah and their ancient stories took root. They had experienced the crisis of exile and now lived under the authority of a series of foreign nations who had conquered their land. First the Persians ruled (from 539 until 332 BCE), then the Greeks (until 164 BCE). After a revolt (led by the Maccabees and still commemorated today at Hanukkah) and a short period of Jewish rule (until 63 BCE), the Romans entered the picture.

Half a millennium of foreign presence raised pressing issues for many Jews wanting to remain faithful to God and his word.

For one thing, the mere presence of foreign rulers in the Holy Land was a bit of an embarrassment: Why would God allow this to happen to us? Does this say something about what he thinks of us? Are we still his people? We already saw in chapter 3 how this frame of mind drove the writer of Chronicles to present a very different story of Israel to address these questions.

With foreign presence also came foreign influence, which caused another sort of soul-searching and conflict among Jews.

Greek and Roman cultures weren't always favorable to those wishing to maintain the laws and customs of Judaism. They might not have been openly hostile to Jewish ways (though there were moments), but just mixing with Greeks and Romans presented temptations to Jews to abandon or at least compromise on their traditions.

With all those factors in play, a pressing question was how to maintain Jewish identity here and now. What does it even mean to be Jewish?

Scripture provided the authoritative answer, but because the world around them was changing—not to mention the diverse views in the Bible, including in the law, as we saw in the last chapter— it wasn't always obvious how the old book with its old ways and old laws could relate.

Think of the U.S. Constitution, America's "binding" ancient document. The Second Amendment gives citizens the right to bear arms. This amendment was adopted in 1791 in the context of the Revolutionary War and also assumed that people used pistols and muskets that took longer to load than it takes us to heat a Pop-Tart.

What does it mean to be "true" to this amendment today, in a context of school shootings and semiautomatic rifles? How the Second Amendment relates to our world today is hotly debated because it is not obvious, yet the old document is still binding for Americans.

As the generations passed, Jews needed to bridge that gap between their past, with its diverse and binding document, and the ever-changing present, to stay connected to what God was saying to them *now* within the pages of their *ancient* scripture.

Bridging this gap required a creative handling of scripture to find deeper meaning than what the words on the page say on the surface.

And by plumbing the depth of scripture, Jews believed they were accessing the deeper mystery of what God was saying to them now. Indeed, it was God himself extending that invitation to them to dig deeper.

Jesus does this very thing in his interpretation of the burning bush story of Exodus. The reason the crowd approved is because these sorts of "deep" readings of the Bible were by Jesus's time par for the course.

Before Jesus came on the scene, different schools of thought had already developed in order to maintain the connection with the past. One group, which we met above, was the Sadducees, temple priests who accepted only Torah as binding. Another group, the group Jesus belonged to, was the Pharisees. They were known for debating legal matters in Torah, and they accepted all the books as binding.

These parties (along with other groups we don't need to go into) could have very sharp disagreements with each other—the burning bush incident above being one example.

Debating the Bible, especially Torah, and coming up with creative readings to address changing times was a mark of faithful Judaism. Jews were not "legalistic" about handling the Law, which is still a common Christian caricature. Even though scripture was God's word and binding, they understood that the Bible—including Torah—was not a rulebook to be followed to the letter at every point.

Remaining faithful to the Bible here and now meant *having to be* flexible. The debates of the day were about *how to be flexible and creative,* not whether scripture was still binding. That was the world Jesus was a part of.

Yet at the same time Jesus earned the label of troublemaker even among his fellow Jews, whether Sadducees or Pharisees. Through his creative handling of his Bible, Jesus drew attention to himself as the true focus of Torah and the rest of scripture. Jesus also had a habit of picking fights with the Jewish authorities of his day to make his point.

A guy like that was bound to attract some negative attention. And he did.

Jesus Messes with the Bible

JESUS'S CREATIVE handling of his Bible often comes out when he is sparring with his fellow Pharisees, sometimes referred to as "teachers of the Law" or "scribes" (as opposed to Sadducees, who were priests).

A popular belief of the day among some Jews was that God would one day send a king from the line of David, a "messiah" who would deliver the Jews from their present state as tenants in their own land under Roman authority. This idea is rooted in that same Old Testament text we looked at in chapter 3, where Nathan promises David that he would have an unbroken lineage from Solomon on sitting on the throne in Jerusalem (2 Samuel 7). Of course, this didn't happen, given the exile to Babylon and then five hundred years of foreign rule.

Still, some Jews believed that God had not given up on them and would one day (hopefully soon) restore the Davidic dynasty. Then his people could pick up where they left off before the Babylonians sacked Jerusalem in 586 BCE. According to the Gospels, Jesus accepted this title of messiah, the Davidic king.

So playing off this expectation of a Davidic messiah, Jesus gets into the following debate that shows how creative Jesus could be with the Bible.

While teaching in the temple, Jesus asks how it's possible that the messiah could actually be *descended* from David. Of course, Jesus, like other Jews, knows full well the messiah would be descended from David. Jesus is just messing with them—he's egging them on, drawing them into a debate so he can drop the hammer.

Jesus quotes Psalm 110, which begins,

The Lord says to my lord,
"Sit at my right hand, until I make your enemies your footstool."

Nothing mysterious or complicated here. The writer of this psalm is speaking in the first line. He says, "The Lord [=God] says to my lord." Who is "my lord"? A king of Israel who is being crowned.

In the second line, the psalmist quotes what God says to this king on his big day: "sit at my right hand," which is a way of saying that the king is God's second in command over Israel. God will then see to it that all the king's enemies become his "footstool" (are vanquished).

But notice what Jesus does. He takes the entire psalm, *including the first line*, as coming from David's lips. That creates an interesting reading of the psalm. Now it's *David* himself saying: "The Lord [God] says to my lord."

David, in other words, is now calling one of his own future descendants "my lord," his superior.

The implication is that this future "lord of David" cannot be an ordinary descendant of David, but someone so worthy of the title "lord" that David himself feels compelled to use it.

Three guesses whom Jesus sees as being worthy of that title, and the first two don't count.

We see here Jesus handling Psalm 110 in a very ancient, creative way. We might think he is "misreading" the first line of Psalm 110—and from the point of view of the writer of the psalm he is, since Psalm 110 doesn't say what Jesus says it says. But in Jesus's day, such creative handling of the psalm to draw out a deeper meaning is perfectly fine.

What would have turned some heads is Jesus's claim that this psalm has something to say about *him*: he is David's descendant *and* David's Lord.

On its own, and on the surface, the psalm doesn't say this. But when Jesus gets a hold of it, it does.

Getting on board with Jesus's interpretations of the Bible can feel like waking up from suspended animation in the year 2525 in a whole new landscape—especially if we start out assuming that Jesus reads his Bible like we do. But that's a bad assumption, and the bottom line for us is twofold.

1. The way Jesus used the Bible, as unusual as it is for us, was understood and accepted back then. The large crowd that heard Jesus talk about Psalm 110 listened "with delight" as Mark tells us. Jesus's creative handling of this psalm was at home in first-century Judaism.

2. Jesus tended to focus his interpretation of the Bible on himself personally or what he was teaching. Drawing attention to himself as David's "Lord" was *not* at home in first-century Judaism.

Christian readers today, who expect Jesus to read the Bible the way they do, have a lot of trouble getting on board with number one. But number two is what got him into trouble with some influential Jewish authorities of his day.

That's Jesus for you. Making people across time upset with him.

While we're on the subject of Jesus creatively using the book of Psalms to talk about himself, here's one more: Jesus's interpretation of Psalm 82 in the Gospel of John. I devoted just one sentence to this psalm in chapter 4 because I was saving it for here—because it's such fun.

Psalm 82 is one of these places in the Old Testament where, as we saw in the last chapter, God is head of a heavenly "divine council."* This psalm is playing off an idea we see elsewhere in the ancient world: each nation has its own gods with a high god over them. Israel's God, the "Most High,"

---

* Some English translations of the Bible avoid "divine council" language to hide the idea that Israelites believed that other gods exist. I think this is a *very* wrong move, because it insulates Christian readers from the Bible and its world—which a few clicks on the Internet or a half hour on the History Channel can demolish pretty quickly.

will punish the members of the divine council for their unjust rule over the nations. As we see in verses 6–7:

> You are gods, children of the Most High, all of you; nevertheless, you shall die like mortals, and fall like any prince.

Though they are gods, they will "die like mortals."

That's the gist of Psalm 82. Jesus, however, reads it differently.

In John 10, a gathered crowd asks Jesus if he is really the messiah. As usual, Jesus doesn't give a straight answer to a simple question. He goes on for a few lines about how God is his Father, and Jesus's true sheep will hear his voice and won't be snatched out of his hand. He ends his comments by saying, "The Father and I are one."

John reports that the crowd has a problem with that last bit about being "one" with God, and so they pick up stones to stone Jesus, which is the proper penalty for blasphemy, for claiming to be God. Jesus responds by quoting verse 6 of Psalm 82:

> Is it not written in your law, "I said, you are gods"? If those to whom the word of God came were called "gods"—and the scripture cannot be annulled—can you say that the one whom the Father has sanctified and sent into the world is blaspheming because I said, "I am God's Son"?

If right there in the Bible God himself can refer to beings as having divine status, the crowd can't stone Jesus for blasphemy for claiming to be one of them.

Feel free to take a moment and clear your head. Do some push-ups or something.

From the point of view of the writer of Psalm 82, what Jesus says isn't what that writer meant. But, once again, from the point of view of Jesus's first-century Jewish world, creative handling of scripture is what you do.

What was troubling—if I may repeat—was that Jesus used scripture to make claims about himself, in these cases that he was superior to David (Psalm 110) and that he was "one" with God his Father (Psalm 82).

And Jesus didn't just do this sort of thing with some psalms. He did it with Torah.

Jesus: Moses 2.0

OBEDIENCE TO TORAH was a serious matter in Jesus's day. Torah, after all, was given by God to the ancient Israelites through Moses on Mount Sinai, a binding contract between God and his people. The pressing question of what it meant to maintain Jewish identity in the midst of Roman culture led to discussions and debates about how best to obey Torah.

Also, in the fairly recent past (less than two hundred years), Jews had been martyred for remaining faithful to Torah in the face of pressure from Gentile oppressors. Continued engagement of Torah and debating with one another to discern God's will honored their memory.

Torah study and debate were an irrevocable part of Jewish life.

Contrary to what some (perhaps many) Christians think, Jesus, as a first-century Jew, was very much a part of this culture. He wasn't "against" the law, and thinking that he was is part of an unfortunate Christian legacy of removing a Jewish Jesus from his Jewish world and making him into someone we might meet at a church social.

In fact, in Matthew's Gospel Jesus says this of Torah:

Do not think I have come to abolish the law or the prophets; I have come not to abolish but to fulfill. For truly I tell you, until heaven and earth pass away, not one letter, not one stroke of a letter, will pass from the law until all is accomplished. Therefore, whoever breaks one of the least of these commandments, and teaches others to do the same, will be called

least in the kingdom of heaven; but whoever does them and teaches them
will be called great in the kingdom of heaven.

Jesus sounds serious about Torah. But as we'll see in a minute, he
wasn't bound by Torah, either.

This passage is part of a long speech by Jesus commonly referred to
as the "Sermon on the Mount"—although, technically it wasn't a sermon,
since no one was bored into a coma listening to it.

More important, the setting of the "sermon" already tells us what's
coming. We have a man on a mountain relaying Torah to people below.
That sounds familiar. Give me a minute. Oh, right! Moses did that on
Mount Sinai.

Matthew, as we saw in chapter 3, styles Jesus as a new Moses. In this
case he is a *new* lawgiver, one with greater authority than the other Jewish
interpreters of the law—even greater than Moses.

Six times Jesus quotes directly from Torah by saying, "You have heard
that it was said in those ancient times" (or the equivalent). And six times
Jesus contrasts what is written in Torah to *his* view: "But I say to you."

According to Jesus, to understand God and his kingdom, Torah as
it stands does not have the final word. It needs to be reshaped. "Fulfilling Torah," ironically, means going beyond the words on the page and to
another level, which is where you find the heart of God. For Jesus, that
meant intensifying the requirements of Torah in places. At times, it meant
going in another direction.

Murder isn't just killing someone physically, as God told Moses. It
includes hate, "murdering" people in your heart, and speaking to them in
abusive language.

Adultery isn't just physical, as God told Moses, but is also sex in your
mind—thinking about what you want to do, deep down in the secret
places of our minds that are seen only by us and God.

In the book of Deuteronomy God told Moses to allow divorce if the husband wished and if the right paperwork was filed. Jesus quotes these words but then declares Moses wasn't strict enough. In contrast to Moses, Jesus teaches that unfaithfulness is the only grounds for divorce.

God told Moses that Israelites were to make solemn oaths to one another in God's name, an ancient version of a binding contract. Jesus said that true followers of God no longer make any oaths at all, in God's name or any other way. They just do what they say they are going to do. Their word is their bond.

God told Moses that justice was carried out tit for tat, "eye for eye, and tooth for tooth." Jesus said, "Not anymore. Turn the other cheek when someone harms you."

God told Moses that the Israelites were to love their neighbor (a fellow Israelite or welcomed foreigners). Israel's enemies, however, would often feel the point of their swords (ask the Canaanites). Jesus said, "Love your enemies and pray for those who persecute you, so that you may be called children of your Father in heaven." The "persecutors" Jesus likely has in mind aren't your mean neighbor or boss, but the Romans—who, like the Canaanites of old, were living in the Holy Land. And in loving your enemies, Jesus says you will be "perfect" like God is (loving "fully" as God loves).

Jesus's views on Torah were not entirely unique to him. He was not the first Jew, for example, to make divorce more difficult or to say that eye-for-an-eye retaliation should not be applied literally. Again, for Jesus to offer his views on Torah—to clarify or even take it to another level—isn't at all remarkable in his day.

For us, however, I simply want to point out that "You have heard that it was said . . . but I say to you . . ." is hard to square with a rulebook view of the Bible.

For Jesus, interpreting *and* respecting Torah meant—when necessary—not following the script, but being creative and adapting the past to speak to changing circumstances in the present. And in some cases, like divorce and oaths, Jesus finds Moses's words to be inadequate and in need of correction.

Speaking of finding parts of Torah inadequate, one more example comes right after the Sermon on the Mount. A potential follower of Jesus wants to bury his father before joining up. Jesus responds, "Follow me, and let the dead bury their own dead."

Jesus wasn't trying to be cute or cryptic. "Honor your mother and father" is the fifth commandment. Failure to bury one's father was a major dishonor, not only because it's just plain idiotic not to bury a dead parent, but Jewish purity laws didn't look kindly upon leaving dead bodies lying around.

Whether or not Jesus was literally telling this guy to not bother burying his father, the larger point is clear: following Jesus is a burning matter and takes priority over the Torah command to honor one's parents.

Again, Jesus isn't throwing Torah in the dumpster, but the urgency of the in-breaking kingdom of heaven takes priority. "Family," as Jesus explains later, is not defined by blood but "whoever does the will of my father."

Jesus respected, even revered, his scripture as any Jew would have in his day. On the other hand, Jesus thinks that what he has to say about what it means to be right with God isn't just laid out in black and white in scripture to be followed to the letter.

Jesus adapts scripture creatively and at times even leaves some of it behind.

Jesus Picks Fights

AT TIMES JESUS goes out of his way to cross lines that Jewish authority figures dare him to cross—like he's trying to make a point about something. He could back down, but he doesn't.

For example, Jesus has this habit of healing people on the Sabbath. Sabbath was a holy day of rest, which meant refraining from any sort of work.

One of the issues that Jews debated was what exactly "work" was. What were you actually barred from doing on the Sabbath? How much effort could you exert before you were "working"? By Jesus's day, Jewish culture already had a tradition of drawing some clear boundaries to guide people in keeping the law.

Some of Jesus's Sabbath-healing episodes in the Gospels make it clear that he was being watched closely to see whether he would cross the line. If the priests and scribes caught him in the act of healing—of "working"—on the Sabbath, Jesus would open himself up to the charge of law breaking.

Knowing this, Jesus went right ahead and did it anyway.

One episode early in Mark's Gospel has Jesus and his disciples walking through a field on the Sabbath, when the disciples begin picking grain. The Pharisees accuse them of doing what is "unlawful," and according to Jewish teaching it *was* unlawful and everyone knew it—including Jesus.

Jesus responds by reminding them of one brief moment in the life of

David: when he and his men were hungry, they entered the sanctuary and helped themselves to the sacred bread there.

First of all, we have here another example of Jesus's creative handling of his Bible. The scene with David doesn't really fit Jesus's situation. It didn't even happen on the Sabbath. Plus David is escaping King Saul's clutches and grabbing food on the go out of necessity. Jesus and his disciples are just roaming through a field on the Sabbath, and the disciples pluck grain because they are hungry.

Jesus zeroes in on his point at the end of this story in Mark. He says that "sabbath was made for humankind, and not humankind for sabbath," which seems to be a way of saying that Sabbath-keeping is not to get in the way of human need, and if it does, the priorities are skewed.

This kind of comment puts Jesus in good company. Several Old Testament prophets also chide Israel for putting the rote practice of the law (specifically, animal sacrifices) over the practice of justice and righteousness (doing right by others). But still, picking grain like this is not a matter of justice and righteousness. Something else is going on.

Jesus ends this debate this way: "the Son of Man is lord even of the Sabbath." Now Jesus claims to have some authority about what Sabbath means and what can or can't be done on it, at least more authority than the legal tradition, which disallowed things like plucking grain.

Jesus is walking on the edge. He isn't obliterating Sabbath, but he is relativizing it. And, you know, if he felt like it, he could have avoided these conflicts altogether by waiting a few hours to pluck grain or maybe just planning ahead with a box lunch to avoid even giving the impression that he was breaking the law. Or, if he wanted to, seeing that he was caught in the act, he could have gone out of his way to make sure his support of Torah was unwavering.

But instead, Jesus uses (creatively) another portion of scripture to undermine the idea of absolute Sabbath-keeping, and then claims to have the authority to make that judgment.

And as all four Gospels point out again and again, the Jewish authorities got more and more annoyed with Jesus over time for things like this.

Jesus also swims against the stream concerning the Old Testament dietary laws.

Both Matthew and Mark relay a story (although differently) where Jesus says, "what goes into you from the outside does not defile, but what comes out of you"—an odd statement, given that dietary laws in Torah are *exactly* about how certain foods entering your body from the outside defile you.

Matthew's Gospel tells us that the Pharisees were offended to hear Jesus say this, and who can blame them? You have to wonder if that wasn't Jesus's point.

Mark's Gospel goes into more detail about how "evil" comes from the inside, like theft, adultery, murder, and so on. He also adds that Jesus was actually declaring that the Old Testament food laws were now null and void.

We need to be a little careful with Mark's version. Most biblical scholars think that Jesus didn't declare food laws null and void. This comment was Mark's own creation written in hindsight and, as we saw in chapter 3, reflects his purpose for writing—specifically, to make sure later Gentile followers of Jesus understood they didn't need to keep those laws.

Also, in the book of Acts (about ten years or so after Jesus's resurrection), early followers of Jesus deal with the topic of food laws for what seems like the *first time* rather than simply referring back to something Jesus explicitly taught. Paul also makes a big deal about dietary laws in the book of Romans, but never hints that he is following Jesus's lead.

Be that as it may, Jesus's confrontation here with Jewish authorities fits his general pattern of getting in people's faces. Jesus isn't simply entering another debate about how to keep Torah. By his inflated rhetoric, Jesus is raising the question of what validity at least some portions of Torah have.

At least, as the Gospels tell us, that is how many Jewish authorities took it. These sorts of things put Jesus on their high alert watch list.

Jesus Was a Human Being

REMEMBER that this book is about the Bible, specifically watching how the Bible behaves without imposing our own expectations on the Bible.

So in this chapter I haven't been trying to say everything about Jesus, what he taught, or what his impact was. I'm only interested here in paying attention to how Jesus used his Bible.

For one thing, watching Jesus interpret his Bible, in his day and age, in his Jewish way, reinforces what we've been seeing all along in this book: the Bible is an ancient book and makes sense if we look at it in ancient ways.

If we read the Bible expecting it to act any other way, we will make a mess of it and, whether we intend to or not, we will show disrespect for the Bible and the God we believe, in his wisdom, gave us the Bible we have.

I mean, if we try to explain Jesus's handling of his Bible in terms of how many Christians today feel the Bible "ought" to be read, Jesus will look like one of my college Bible students, playing free association with the Bible. Or worse, we may try to find some way of taking Jesus out of his ancient Jewish world and making him look more like a suburban Protestant, an urban hipster, a tea party spokesman, and so on.

In my experience, the latter happens far too often in Christian circles. And it's always a bad move to invent a Jesus who agrees with us rather than challenges us.

Watching Jesus handle his Bible hits us square in the face with the central mystery of the Christian faith. In Jesus, God and man came together in a way that Christians believe they never had before and never will again. That "union" is indeed a mystery, and if you're waiting for me to explain it, you might as well wait for me to explain the Kardashian sisters or why *The Real Housewives of New Jersey* wasn't canceled after the pilot.

But one thing I will say is that Jesus as God-man carries with it certain implications, one of which is that Jesus is not only "fully divine" as the Christian church believes (and tends to focus on), but also "fully human."

And by "fully human," I mean *fully*.

Christians too often forget or push to the side that second part.

If Jesus really was human (and I can't believe I'm even talking like this; of course he was), he was part of actual human history—not in general or in the abstract or at a distance, but a human at a particular point in time and place, with customs, beliefs, expectations.

The Jesus Christ of the Christian faith, to be truly the Jesus Christ that Christians say they confess, *must* be truly and "particularly" (not generally) human.

In other words, without a Jesus who is deeply part of the world of first-century Judea—as anyone at the time would be—there can be no true Christian confession that Jesus is God *and* human *mysteriously* in one.

In this chapter, we simply applied that line of thought about Jesus to one topic: how Jesus handled his Bible as a Jew in the first century CE. Jesus handled his Bible in a "fully human" (i.e., first-century Jewish) way.

Christians may want a Jesus who is unique or stands out in every way, at every moment, who keeps his distance from the "human" drama, but that is not the way it works. We may want a Jesus who doesn't get creative with his Bible but gets it "right" (which usually means "who does things the way I expect him to").

But when God enters the human drama, he's all in.

As inconvenient, even disturbing, as that may be, that is what the New Testament calls "Good News."

The Gospels, of course, have a lot more to say about Jesus, and, as we saw in chapter 3, the four Gospels present Jesus differently. The Gospel writers wrote a generation and more after Jesus's life, and they wrote about him not simply as a part of past history but how that itinerant preacher was with them now in the present.

They had faith that Jesus was the risen Son of God, and their stories of Jesus, though different, reflected that faith.

Working out how these four portraits of Jesus work together to present Jesus to us fills shelves with thick books. Still, when I read the Gospels, one word sums up what I see about Jesus as a whole: counterintuitive.

A working-class man whose words and deeds were of resounding authority, wisdom, and cleverness, enough to capture the negative attention of the Jewish authorities and the Roman government.

A leader who modeled self-sacrifice and service to others instead of power.

A deliverer who suffered and was executed, whose power was shown through weakness. Glory through ignobility.

That's the paradox of the Christian faith, and it's always been hard to take in. In the early years of the Jesus movement, one follower of Jesus in particular, the apostle Paul, would take up the task of explaining this paradox.

And in doing so, Paul would find himself rethinking Israel's entire story, from beginning to end, transforming it from a story of an ethnically distinct people into a message for every nation, with even cosmic implications.

Under Paul, Israel's story will bend its knee to King Jesus, the risen Son of God. A fully Christian way of reading the Bible is born.

No One Saw This Coming

I Could Tell You But You Wouldn't Understand

AS I WRITE THIS, my daughter recently upgraded to an iPhone 5, which, I'm told is "way better" than the iPhone 4, but all I know is it costs me more and chains me to another two-year contract. And it never ends. The iPhone 6 came out as I was finishing the last sentence. By the time this book gets published we should be seeing the iPhone 17, which I'm told will read minds and clone itself.

My cell phone doesn't talk to me, can't download music or videos, and doesn't come with an atlas of every town on Earth. I'm fine with that. When I was young (here it comes), we didn't even *have* cell phones. Our phones were bolted to the kitchen wall with a coiled cord connecting the talking part to the dialing part. And then we walked to school uphill both ways in a snowstorm, and we liked it that way, dagnabbit.

Techy families had newfangled push-button phones that beeped and had really long cords so you could move way into the other room for some privacy. We started seeing "car phones" when I was in high school. They were the size of carry-on luggage and made us laugh.

And to think it all started in 1876, when Alexander Graham Bell uttered to his assistant Thomas Watson the first words carried by tele-phone, "Mr. Watson, come here, I want to see you." I don't quite get the subdued formality ("Tom!!! Get in here!! Holy . . . OMG . . . It *works*!!"), but I digress. That first call traveled between adjoining rooms. By 1892 Bell placed a call from New York to Chicago, and in 1915 Bell called Watson in San Francisco. This was huge, and we are all—my daughter included—in Bell's debt.

I sometimes wonder—since I apparently have so little to do—what it would be like to go back in time with the latest iPhone and explain it to Bell, to bring a little bit of the future into Bell's world, to show him where his idea would end up.

To state the obvious, Bell would have no frame of reference for an iPhone. It's made of plastic (?!) and fits in your pocket. No wires. It bounces signals (?!) off satellites (?!) orbiting (?!) the earth. It has apps, memory, and ten-hour batteries the size of an aspirin. And if that weren't enough to take in, a few taps on a touch screen gives you virtually instant access to any bit of information past or present anywhere in the world. It can even hold a conversation with you.

My only chance of getting Bell to grasp this otherworldly future phone would be by adapting his older language as best I could. I'd need to talk about the iPhone's circuits, memory, and wireless capability in terms of wires, switchboards, and hand cranks. I'm not sure how I'd explain downloading, Angry Birds, or Justin Bieber videos, but one thing at a time.

Bell seems like he was a pretty bright guy, but at the end of the day—and I think we all know this—the concepts and language of Bell's world weren't set up to handle this utterly surprising bit of the future that invaded his present. I would need to get creative in using Bell's familiar language to describe something it was never intended to describe.

The story of Jesus is connected to the story of Israel like the iPhone is connected to Bell's original. Israel's story began it all, and without it there would be no Jesus story.

But Jesus's story also brings with it something utterly new and unexpected that Israel's story is not set up to handle.

Jesus's story is deeply connected to Israel's story yet has a surprise ending. If we miss this paradox, we will miss seeing how the earliest Christian writers creatively adapted the familiar language of their Bible (the Christian Old Testament) to talk about Jesus. They believed Israel's story was God's Word, but what Jesus said and did could not be explained by that story.

To talk about Jesus they *had* to adapt and transform the old language for a new task.

Watching the New Testament writers at work yields a valuable lesson for Christian readers today: explaining Jesus drove the early Christian writers to read their Bible in new, sometimes radically different, ways.

The Bible was nonnegotiable as God's word, but it wasn't God's *final* word. Jesus was.

Israel's story, taken on its own terms, is not adequate to bear the weight of God's surprise move of a crucified and resurrected messiah. It must be reshaped around Jesus.

If we miss that lesson—if we look to the Bible as a collection of unchanging information about God and miss how the reality of Jesus *necessarily* transforms Israel's story—we will miss what the earliest Christian writers have to say.

We will miss Jesus.

Good News! Our Leader Was Executed by the Romans! Come Join Us!

JESUS WAS CRUCIFIED on Good Friday and raised from the dead on the third day, on Easter Sunday.

Christians today reading this hardly break stride. It's Christianity 101. Crucified and resurrected. Got it. Move on. But for a first-century Jewish audience, shaped by its ancient story, an executed and resurrected messiah was utterly unexpected and completely outside their frame of reference.

We can see an example of this in the Gospels. When Jesus told his disciples that he would suffer, die, and be raised from the dead three days later, Peter took Jesus aside and reamed him out. Jesus shot back, "Get behind me, Satan! You are a stumbling block to me; for you are setting your mind not on divine things but on human things."

Jesus could have been a bit easier on Peter, I suppose, but this exchange illustrates how absurd a dying and rising messiah was to those who first heard about it. No one saw it coming.

The general idea of "messiah" was familiar to first-century Jews, though various opinions were held about what this figure would do. One of those views, as we glimpsed in the last chapter, was that the messiah would be a king in the line of David—a "Davidic messiah"—who would reestablish Israel's political and religious independence. That idea grew out of Israel's story itself (namely Nathan's prophecy in 2 Samuel 7), and, as we read in the Gospels, some Jews seemed to think Jesus might be the one who would pull it off. Certainly, the New Testament makes a lot out of Jesus being a Davidic messiah, which we'll get to in a minute.

But Jesus didn't pull off what a Davidic messiah was expected to pull off. Instead of defeating the Romans, he was executed by them, hung on a wooden cross as a common criminal. Alone this wouldn't have raised an eyebrow. He simply met the same fate as other would-be Jewish liberators had. Just check him off the Davidic messiah candidate list, forget about him, and keep your eyes open for a burly and chiseled warrior-king.

But the early followers of Jesus also believed that Israel's God vindicated this executed messiah by raising him from the dead.

Now things get interesting—and getting a handle on this makes all the difference in how Christians think of their Bible, Jesus, and what the first followers of Jesus meant when they said "Good News."

Like "messiah," the basic idea of "resurrection" wasn't new. Many Jews in Jesus's day believed that God would one day in the future raise from the dead and reward all faithful Jews.

After all, for centuries Jews had lived and died waiting for God to show up to deliver them from foreign oppression, especially from the Greeks and now the Romans. Some had been martyred for their steadfast faith, so it's only right that a faithful God would return the favor by raising them from the dead in order to include them in the "world to come," as it was called.

But the resurrection *of Jesus* was an unexpected twist. Rather than raising *all* faithful Jews one day in the *future,* the early followers of Jesus claimed that God had pulled a fast one: he raised *one* Jew *now.* Why would Israel's God do *this* instead of sticking to the plan? What in the world was happening!?

It took a while, but the early followers of Jesus began to put the pieces together. Resurrection is a future thing, part of the "world to come." Raising Jesus now meant that the "world to come" was already here—at least a preview of it.

A bit of the future had broken into the present, and so a new era had dawned.

An executed messiah, raised from the dead, pushing the "world to come" into the present. This is how Jesus's followers claimed that Israel's God was on the move during the days of Roman rule. To be a part of this new world that Jesus launched, one needed to pledge allegiance to Jesus as God's Son, God's chosen messiah—to put their trust in Jesus, to have faith, to believe.

A future world invading the present took some getting used to in Jesus's day, as it does now. The New Testament writers, trying to wrap their arms around the idea, found different ways of taking a stab at it.

The apostle Paul talks as if God had pressed reset and all creation got a cosmic do-over: "So if anyone is in Christ, there is a new creation: everything old has passed away; see, everything has become new!" John's Gospel calls it being "born from above" (by God's power), or "born again" as the apostle Peter puts it—a personal do-over in addition to the cosmic one Paul wrote about.

And if that's not enough of a twist, here's another—and it's a big one. These early Christians, especially the apostle Paul, claimed this new world that was opened by Jesus, the *Jewish* messiah, was equally open to *everyone,* Jew or Gentile.

In raising this Jesus from the dead, Paul argued, Israel's God had put on display a major shift: "Chosen People" now included those who weren't previously the Chosen People—the Gentiles. God had flung the door open and now everyone was invited to the party, just as they are. Jews and Gentiles were now on equal footing before God.

For any Jew who saw him or herself as one of the Chosen People, hearing a claim like this would have been hard to take in—frankly, it would have sounded ridiculous, as if God was turning his back on their unique tradition, their rich heritage, their story—the story God himself had written.

What we've got here is more than just a slight adjustment to Israel's story.

Jesus's earliest followers had what seems like an almost impossible task of explaining how *Israel's* God could show up in such a—how should I put it—non-Israelite, unbiblical, unexpected way. And this brings us to the writers of the New Testament, and especially Paul.

Now, this next part brings us to the main point of this chapter. And it's important—so important I am going to use exclamation points at the end of this sentence to make you stop for a moment and think, *Hey, I bet what's coming up is important.*

!!!!!!

Jesus, as I've been saying, was a surprise ending that could not be adequately expressed in the old language of Israel's story. But these early followers of Jesus couldn't toss out the script, nor would it remotely enter their minds to do so. Like Jesus himself, they were Jewish (at least most of them). Israel's story was *their* story, and the God of Israel was the *same God* responsible for this surprise ending.

Israel's story was the only God-talk these Jewish followers of Jesus had available to them. So what did they do? They *adapted and transformed* their sacred story to serve the story of Jesus—the story of the future invading the present, of an executed and raised messiah, of a "new creation."

These writers did not fret about sticking to the biblical script. They couldn't, and they knew it. Scripture became more of a jumping-off point for talking about something the old language wasn't set up to handle. And—even more so than Jesus in the last chapter—they got pretty creative about it, too.

Readers today who expect these writers to "stick to the Bible," as if that was their main concern, are often perplexed when reading how these writers actually handle the Old Testament. What they say can look random, disconnected, and even bizarre.

But rather than me talking about it, let's let these early Christian writers speak for themselves. And here are a few more exclamation points to remind you how important all this is and to pause for a moment before you move on to the next page to see the New Testament writers at work.

!!!!!!

"It's All About Me."—Jesus
(According to Luke and Matthew)

IN THE LAST CHAPTER of Luke's Gospel (the only Gospel that contains this story), Jesus meets up with his disciples after his resurrection. The disciples were huddled together and freaking out a bit. Their leader had been executed two days earlier, which was unsettling enough. But now they were starting to hear reports that Jesus wasn't dead at all, but walking around and talking to people.

While they were pondering all this, Jesus appeared out of nowhere. True to form, the dim-witted disciples, a truly confused group of individuals, had no idea what was going on. They thought Jesus was a ghost and so freaked out further. Jesus proved he was no ghost by showing them his wounds and by eating some fish. That seemed to work, since only in Harry Potter books do ghosts have wounds and eat. Then Jesus explained to them what was going on:

"I'm not sure why you're so surprised. I've been telling you for years that everything that's happened here these last few days follows what scripture says—the books of Moses, the books of the prophets, the Psalms, every part of it. But since you are having so much trouble grasping what I said, let me spell it out for you—again. Read your Bible: there you will find that *I had to suffer and die, and that I would rise from the dead on the third day.*"

It's all right there in black and white.

Only, it isn't—which brings me to my point.

You can read the Old Testament as carefully and as often as you want—standing on your head, backward, with special decoder glasses, or in Klingon—and you won't find anything about a future messiah *dying and rising from the dead on the third day,* the very thing Jesus says you *will* find there. Not a word. Don't even bother looking.

So what's Luke's angle? Why does Jesus say something is in the Bible when it clearly isn't? That makes no sense.

No, it doesn't—until we are clear on what Jesus is actually telling his disciples.

Jesus didn't mean for the disciples to root through their Bibles to find the places where a dying-and-rising-from-the-dead messiah was hiding—like a first-century *Where's Waldo?*

Jesus isn't "in" Israel's story that way. You'll never read Israel's story on its own terms and "find Jesus" on the surface.

To see Jesus, you won't get there by sticking to the script. You will only see Jesus there in hindsight and under the surface, where your reading of the Old Testament is *driven* by faith in Christ, where Jesus has become the starting point for re-understanding Israel's story, not the logical conclusion of Israel's story.

Here in Luke's Gospel Jesus is not telling his disciples to stick literally to the script. He is telling them to reread the script in light of his death and resurrection.

When you do that, Jesus says, you will come to understand that Israel's story is *no longer* a book primarily about Israel, but a book that now speaks of Jesus as the center and focus of Israel's story, the final chapter that ties together Israel's long difficult journey through history.

Jesus is what the Old Testament is "about," which is not an obvious way of reading it. So Luke adds that Jesus "opened their minds" so the disciples could understand Israel's story in the new Jesus way. Luke doesn't flesh out for his readers right here exactly how Jesus is the focus of Israel's story. The rest of Luke's Gospel takes care of that, and we'll get to a big example below.

Let's look at Matthew's Gospel, to see this Jesus focus of the Old Testament from a different angle.

As we saw in chapter 3, the story of Jesus's birth in Matthew's Gospel includes a scene of wicked King Herod's murderous rampage. The Magi "from the East" come to Herod led by a star looking for a child "born king of the Jews."

Apparently these "wise men" have no clue that Herod would naturally see this as a threat. And so, not wanting any competition, Herod orders a mass slaying of all male infants just to make sure he gets the right one. But the angel of the Lord warns Joseph in a dream to sneak his family out of town and live in Egypt until Herod dies. Then they could come back.

That's the story: the infant Jesus is brought to Egypt for safety and then later returns home.

If Matthew had left it at that we wouldn't blink an eye. But Matthew adds an odd twist—odd at least for modern readers—which shows us how deeply he had rethought Israel's story and centered it around Jesus.

Matthew said that Jesus's journey to Egypt and back home again "fulfilled" the words of the eighth century BCE Old Testament prophet Hosea, who wrote: "Out of Egypt I called my son." So according to Matthew, the return of Jesus (God's Son) from Egypt is predicted by the prophet Hosea about seven hundred years earlier.

Only it's not.

In the eighth century BCE, the issue on the table for Hosea was the disobedience of the northern kingdom (this was after the division of Israel into north and south about two hundred years earlier). That disobedience would soon lead to the exile of the northern kingdom by the mighty Assyrians in 722 BCE.

When Hosea, speaking for God (as prophets do), says, "Out of Egypt I called my son," he isn't *predicting* something that would happen hundreds of years in the *future* to *one person* (Jesus). Hosea is *reminiscing,* looking *back* hundreds of years to the time when God rescued his "son" *Israel* from Egyptian slavery. Hosea goes on to say that Israel showed its thanks to God—after all God had done for them—by worshipping the Canaanite god Baal.

Matthew used Hosea's words in a way that Hosea absolutely did not mean, and in a way Hosea would never, in a million years, have understood. Today we would call this reading "into" the text what we want to see there. And this is exactly what Matthew is doing. His faith in Jesus drove him to adapt Israel's story to speak about Jesus, even if Jesus is off topic from the point of view of Hosea's own words.

Matthew wasn't a stupid reader, and he didn't just pull a portion of the Old Testament out of thin air. Matthew was a creative reader of his Bible—as we saw of Jesus in the last chapter, and as was par for the course in the Judaism of the day.

As we glimpsed in chapter 3, part of Matthew's creative telling of Jesus's birth story is to present him as a new Moses. Both Jesus and Moses escape a mass-murdering monarch—Pharaoh was threatened by the Hebrew reproduction rate, ordered the male infants to be drowned in the Nile, and Moses alone escaped in a basket on the Nile. Then as an adult, Moses again escapes Pharaoh's wrath for killing an Egyptian.

Moses only returns, as the book of Exodus tells us, after God told him that, "all those who were seeking your life are dead." These are the very same words that God tells Joseph in Matthew: the holy family is to return home "for those who were seeking the child's life are dead."

Matthew "hooks" his portrait of Jesus as the new and improved Moses onto this passage in Hosea. The fact that Israel is called God's "son" in Hosea also invited Matthew to connect creatively that moment from the past to Jesus, whom Matthew believed to be God's "Son."

For Matthew, whose audience probably had a large Jewish Christian component, Jesus and Israel mirror each other: both are God's "son" chosen for a divine purpose.

The further details of what exactly Matthew means by appealing to Hosea to talk about Jesus is interesting and all, but I want to make a much simpler point here: for Matthew, what Hosea meant back then isn't what Hosea's words ultimately and *really* mean. Jesus has come and so Israel's story is now transposed to talk about Jesus. That is Matthew's conviction, his starting point, and he rereads his Bible accordingly.

The need to explain Jesus as both surprise ending *and* deeply connected to Israel's story drove the Gospel writers to do some creative reading.

Sticking to what the Bible says wasn't their goal.

Talking about Jesus was.

Are We There Yet?

ALL FOUR GOSPEL WRITERS transform one key moment in Israel's story around Jesus: the exile to Babylon and Israel's return.

In Jesus's day, the exile had been over for about five hundred years, but a problem remained. As long as a foreign power, namely the Romans, was in control of the land God had given to Israel long ago, things are not as they should be—the exile, in a sense, was not completely over.

It's like coming home from a long vacation only to find the government had seized your house and let others move in. You're home but not really home until the usurpers are driven out and you can go back to living in your house as before.

For some Jews at the time, a Davidic messiah was expected to correct this problem, to restore Israel fully in the land by being in charge of it like it was back in the old days. That meant reclaiming the Israelites' land and their capital, Jerusalem, which further meant getting rid of the Romans somehow. And when that true liberation came, all the nations would see it and acknowledge Israel's God as the one and only God. That's the plan, at least, and the Davidic messiah would lead the way.

We get a quick glimpse of how ingrained this plan was from a story in Mark's Gospel involving two of Jesus's disciples, brothers James and John. On the way to Jerusalem, where Jesus would be executed about a week later, they pull Jesus to the side and ask if they could sit at his right and left side when he enters his "glory."

They're not talking about going to heaven after they die. They're talking about politics. They want to be King Jesus's second in command when he is crowned king in Jerusalem. That's what they think they are heading to Jerusalem to do.

The other disciples overhear this little plan, and tempers start flaring. Jesus nips it all in the bud by explaining to them, for the umpteenth time, that he is not going to Jerusalem to take over but to die. And if they really want to "rule" with him, they need to be willing to follow his lead and become *servants* of each other.

After all that time with Jesus, the idea of a messiah doing anything other than seizing control over Jerusalem was still bizarre for his closest, handpicked followers. If I had been there, I'm sure I would have been right there with them.

The Gospel writers jump all over the idea of a Davidic messiah bringing a complete end to the exile and use it to explain Jesus—which is interesting, because Jesus wanted nothing to do with restoring Israel's glory days of political independence.

And with that we come to our point.

The Gospel writers *redefined* the familiar idea of "exile" and what it meant for that exile to come to an end. Rather than ending in political triumph, Israel's story now gets rewritten around Jesus into a very different kind of exile-and-return story. Familiar language is transformed to explain the unexpected. And you only need to read the first page of the New Testament to see it.

The Gospel of Matthew begins with a list of names from Israel's ancestor Abraham to Jesus. Admittedly, beginning the story of the central figure in Christian history with a list of names is a bit of a snoozer, but put the remote down and give the guy a chance.

Matthew's Gospel, like the others, is a well-thought-out and carefully written portrait of Jesus. He's not winging it. He's got a plan. At least hear him out.

His list of names is a setup. He is using the familiar language of "ending the exile" only to switch directions entirely a bit further down.

Matthew clearly spells out that his genealogy of Jesus has three segments: *Abraham* to *David; David* to the *Exile;* the *Exile* to *Jesus.* First of all, the very fact that Matthew lists "exile" in a genealogy tells us he's up to something; genealogies are about people, not events. "Exile" sounds like it might be important here.

Also, each segment, Matthew goes out of his way to tell us, has fourteen names. Why fourteen? It's not his lucky Lotto number. Matthew is saying something about Jesus's significance.

Note that David is prominently featured: he ends the first segment and begins the second. The name David in Hebrew has a numerical value of— wait for it—fourteen. (Ancient Hebrew had no written number system, so consonants were used as numbers. D is 4 and V is 6 so DaViD = 14.)

Matthew's genealogy isn't like the accurate ancestry record you'd find in a county courthouse today (and compare Matthew's genealogy to Luke's to see two very different takes on Jesus's ancestry). Matthew's genealogy is creatively and carefully crafted to present Jesus as Israel's long-awaited deliverer—descended from *David,* who will bring an *end to the exile* and restore the land promised long ago to *Abraham.*

In that Jewish world of the first century, the point of Matthew's message would have been grasped easily enough: the days of Roman rule are numbered and liberation is around the corner. But Matthew only introduces his Jesus story like this. As we keep reading, we see that Matthew is quickly going to adjust the old and familiar expectations to fit the surprise ending.

Take the Sermon on the Mount. Here is Jesus's first big public appearance, according to Matthew, and he tells the gathered Jewish crowd that the *meek* will inherit the earth, the *peacemakers* are God's true children, and the *persecuted* are the ones inside of God's kingdom.

Jesus isn't telling the crowd to play nice and share their toys. He is alerting them that no one should expect him to wage a retaliatory strike against the Romans. He's not that kind of messiah. Matthew's Jesus will redefine what Israel's exile is all about and what it means to bring it to its full end. Rather than a Davidic king sitting on the throne in Jerusalem over a national/political entity, Matthew will transform these familiar ideas and take his readers into uncharted territory.

Let's back up a page or two and bring John the Baptist into this. His job is to announce the appearance of Jesus as a public figure. All four Gospels call him a "voice crying in the wilderness" who cries out "prepare the way of the Lord." These words come straight from the same section in the book of Isaiah, where God speaks words of comfort to the Israelites *in exile in Babylon*. God is on the move and soon the exile will end. So "prepare the way of the Lord." It's time to come home.

All four Gospels use *these words* from Isaiah to introduce the story of Jesus. So we're not going too far out on a limb by concluding that whatever Jesus is going to do has something to do with bringing an end to the exile—though, again, not according to expectations.

Matthew ends his Gospel with another twist on the exile story. In the Old Testament, the future of Israel includes the nations coming *to* Jerusalem to embrace Israel and Israel's God. But Matthew's "end of exile" story ends differently.

After the resurrection, Jesus commissions his disciples, saying "All authority in heaven and on earth has been given to me. *Go* therefore and make disciples of all nations, baptizing them in the name of the Father and of the Son and of the Holy Spirit, and teaching them to obey everything that I have commanded you."

This is how Israel's exile comes to an end for Matthew—not by restoring Israel's kingdom as in the days of David. Rather, Jerusalem and the land of Israel are no longer God's focal points. The disciples are to leave their land and make disciples from all nations, teaching them to follow Jesus and what he (not Moses) commanded, spreading the word of a different kind of kingdom and a different kind of king.

Not at all what Israel's story imagined, but things are different now. Jesus has come, and now Israel's story is transformed.

Jesus, Savior of the ~~Jews~~ World

THE BEGINNING of Luke's Gospel also transforms "end of exile" language, though differently than Matthew does with his genealogy.

In the story of Jesus's birth, the angel Gabriel announces to Mary that she will bear a son. He will be *"Son of the Most High,"* will be given *"the throne of his ancestor David,"* and his kingdom will have *"no end."*

To Christian ears, the meaning of these words gets lost in how the story of Jesus will end—with his resurrection. So Christians tend to hear a clear echo of Jesus being the *divine* Son of God who will rise, ascend to his heavenly throne, and reign in heaven forever.

But Luke hasn't gotten there yet, and we shouldn't jump ahead too quickly.

In Israel's ancient world, kings ruled as divine stand-ins and so were called "sons" of a deity. One of the psalms (Psalm 2) also describes the anointing of a king of Israel (probably David) that way: "You are my son; today I have begotten you." To become a king of Israel means to be "begotten" (to be fathered) as a "son of God" in a symbolic sense.

Referring to Jesus as "Son of the Most High" is Israelite king language.

Next, to sit on David's *throne* in a kingdom with *no end* echoes the promise to David from 2 Samuel we saw in chapter 3. God told David that his line of descendants, beginning with Solomon, would rule perpetually in Jerusalem. But that perpetual line was broken during the exile in Babylon, which is just one reason why the exile was so tragic to Israelite consciousness. Things had gotten so bad that God actually broke his earlier promise.* Now many Jews were looking for a time when God would renew that promise: a king in the line of David to come along and pick up right where they left off. No harm, no foul.

So if you never heard of Jesus or Christianity and read Luke talking about the birth of a son of God, who will sit on David's throne and resume the unbroken royal line, you would draw a perfectly Jewish conclusion: Luke thinks Jesus is the long-awaited king of Israel who will deliver his people from the enemy and reestablish the kingdom of Israel in Jerusalem.

That's certainly what Mary got out of it.

While visiting her pregnant relative Elizabeth (mother of John the Baptist), Mary bursts into prayer about how God has blessed her with a child, and how God is going to raise up the lowly and cut the powerful down to size, feed the hungry and make the rich go away empty.

At the end of her prayer, Mary gets very specific.

He [God] has helped his servant Israel, in remembrance of his mercy, according to the promise he made to our ancestors, to Abraham and to his descendants forever.

Mary's prayer, like Gabriel's announcement, is Israel centered. She expects that God is about to fulfill his promise to Abraham and the ancestors in the form of a liberator to deliver Israel—which at the moment means from under Roman oppression.

It helps to know that Mary's prayer looks oh so similar to the prayer in the Old Testament of another happy mother, Hannah. Like Mary, Hannah received a son by God's intervention. Her son Samuel would grow up to be the powerful prophet who would later anoint (guess who) David as Israel's

---

* If you want to see how upset the Israelites were with God about breaking his promise, Psalm 89 lays it out there. This psalm accuses God of turning his back on Israel and hiding. (How can anyone *not* like a Bible that gets in God's face like this?)

king. Hannah offers a long prayer of thanks to God about how God is going to come to Israel's rescue and shatter its enemies through this anointed king.

The overlap between the prayers of these two special mothers is easy to see if you lay them side by side, and it isn't a coincidence. Luke fashions Mary's prayer to mimic the prayer of Hannah. Mary's son is going to embody the ancient hope of a powerful and godly David-like ruler in Jerusalem who will restore the kingdom, deliver the people, and bring peace.

Next in Luke's story we meet Zechariah, the father of John the Baptist. At the birth of his son, Zechariah praises God for how Israel's oppressors (the Romans) are about to face the music. A "mighty savior" from David's line is on his way. Through him, God will have "mercy" on the Israelites by delivering them from "our enemies," from "all who hate us." Then Jews will be able to worship God once again in their temple, on their land, "without fear." Short version: Zechariah expects that it's payback time for the Romans.

Next, old man Simeon sees the baby Jesus and is thankful to God that he let him live long enough to see the "Lord's messiah." Simeon expects that this messiah would bring the "consolation of Israel"—which is straight-down-the-middle Old Testament talk for restoring Israel after the exile. Simeon also borrows words from the prophet Isaiah: all the world, all the Gentiles, will see this "salvation" of Israel by God's hand. Israel will once again hold top spot on the list of nations.

Finally, we meet old Anna, a widowed prophet, who fasted at the temple day and night. On seeing the baby Jesus, she praises God and declares that the child would bring about the "redemption of Jerusalem"— meaning, the deliverance of Jerusalem from foreign rule.

Gabriel, Mary, Elizabeth, Zechariah, Simeon, and Anna, in the first two chapters of Luke's Gospel, all talk about Jesus as delivering on God's ancient promises—the final end of the exile.

Luke plays on this expectation, and the echoes are clear as a church bell on a midwinter's night. But soon Luke's Jesus begins to say and do very un-messiah-like things.

We already see a preview of this when Gabriel tells Mary that God's spirit will "overshadow" her, thus causing her to get pregnant. This little bit of information is an early sign in Luke's Gospel that *this* messiah isn't going to be confined to old categories—he is God's "son" on a different level.

Luke also seems to be throwing a hard right uppercut at the idea of Roman kingship. As we saw in chapter 3, official Roman policy held that Caesar Augustus (the Caesar at Jesus's birth) was begotten of the gods, sent to the people as a gift to restore "peace," to "save" the people, and to bring "good news." Luke uses these same words to describe Jesus's birth.

Jesus not only breaks the mold of Jewish political ideas, but Roman as well. Jesus is super-Caesar.

As Luke's story unfolds, Jesus continues to undermine expectations involving political power and Jewish identity. In his first public appearance, in a synagogue service, he claims to be the messiah, which creates quite a buzz of support—until he tells them that he will bless Gentiles and be rejected by his own kinsmen. The crowd responds by trying to throw Jesus off a cliff. Israel's messiah isn't supposed to say things like this.

Then later, in one of Jesus's more unmessianic moments, he forgives people's sins, which is only something God can do. Jesus was immediately charged with blasphemy—not something a would-be messiah wants on his résumé.

The more familiar you are with Jewish expectations at the time, the more your head explodes by the time you get to the end of Luke's Gospel. Israel's messiah doesn't regroup and follow through with the plan. He suffers defeat on a Roman cross, and then—as if things couldn't get any weirder—he walks out of his tomb three days later.

In part two of Luke's story, the book of Acts, the return from exile has become a universal story—much like how Matthew ends his Gospel with messengers going out into all the world to make disciples of Jesus from every nation. The book of Acts relays how the gospel spread from a few frightened disciples to Asia Minor, Greece, and then the nerve center of the empire, Rome itself, in about thirty years.

The idea of Israel's full "return" to the land was transformed by the Gospel writers to speak about Jesus and God's unexpected move—a crucified and risen messiah. The Gospel writers used the language of Israel's script but infused that language with a whole new meaning.

*   *   *

More than any other writer of the New Testament, the apostle Paul transforms Israel's story—beyond even where Jesus and the Gospel writers took it.

A centerpiece of Paul's letters is that the Good News of the Jewish messiah Jesus is for everyone, and by everyone he means Jews *and Gentiles.* Paul argued that Gentiles could be *fully* part of the family of *Israel's* God just the way they are, *as Gentiles,* without adopting Jewish laws and traditions first. The idea was radical enough to ruffle the feathers of even some of Jesus's other followers (Paul mentions in the book of Galatians a run-in with Peter).

Jesus was a surprise ending; a crucified and risen messiah wasn't something Israel's story was set up to handle. Yet, for Paul, *this* is how *Israel's* God was now moving in the world.

To get this radical idea across, Paul had to reimagine his scripture, transforming it from a local and ethnic story into a universal story around Jesus. Paul even wound up declaring parts of Israel's story null and void.

If you are expecting Paul to read the Bible like it was set in stone, you will find yourself getting pretty nervous. For Paul, now that Jesus has come, the Bible was more like clay to be molded.

God's Answer to a Question No One Was Asking

PAUL WOUND UP WRITING most of the New Testament, but he wasn't sold on Jesus at first. He started out as a devout Jew; some might say a bit over the top. In the book of Acts, Luke describes Paul as a thug. He hated that good Jews were duped into following this Jesus character, so, to serve God, he rounded them up and threw them into prison—which, given what we can gather of Paul's personality, was likely his dream job.

Nothing personal. It's just business.

Following a false messiah meant potentially missing the real one when he comes, which would be one big fat disaster. And for any self-aware Jew who knew something about Israel's story, especially an educated Jew like Paul, Jesus was beyond the shadow of a doubt, without question, no need to discuss, a false messiah: he was executed by the bad guys (he lost), in fact crucified on a wooden cross like a common criminal. He also had a reputation for not playing ball with the Jewish authorities and being soft on the legal system.

According to the book of Acts, now that Jesus was safely dead and buried, Paul thought it was time to clean up the whole unfortunate episode by going after anyone who had somehow been fooled into thinking that

Jesus was the real deal. We read that Paul even got permission from the high priest in Jerusalem to go far north to the synagogues in Damascus and drag these Jesus followers back to Jerusalem to face justice.

On the way, as Luke tells us, Jesus appeared to Paul in a blast of light and spoke to him, which rattled Paul a bit, blinded him, and resulted in a major career change only slightly less dramatic than Rush Limbaugh joining the Democratic Party.

From now on Paul, of all people, would be a follower of Jesus and charged with the heretofore unimaginable task of spreading the message of Jesus not only to his fellow Jews but beyond Jewish boundaries to the Gentiles.

In one of his letters, Paul says that he left the area for three years to sort all this out before returning to Jerusalem. And he did have a lot to sort out. Not only did Paul have to deal with why God's messiah didn't follow the plan, he also had to wrap that brilliant head of his around a pretty basic question, when you stop to think about it.

Aborting the messiah playbook was one thing. God can do what he wants. But why would God abort it *this way specifically,* with an executed and raised-from-the-dead messiah? Why did God show up like *this*?

If a dying and rising messiah, as surprising as it was, is God's solution, what exactly is he solving? What is the problem that needs this kind of messiah?

If this Jesus is God's answer, what is the question?

Paul eventually came to the conclusion that God was answering a question that gets at the core of not simply the Jewish drama, but the human drama, a question that no one was yet asking in quite the same way.

Breaking Torah was the problem that landed the Israelites in exile in the first place a few centuries earlier. The fact that the Romans were now walking around like they owned the place (because they did) meant—as we've seen—that Israel's place in the world is not yet fully restored: the full effects of the exile are not yet dealt with.

If unfaithfulness to Torah resulted in exile, and if the exile is not completely over, logically there must still be a lingering Torah-breaking problem that had to be addressed.

So being unfaithful to Torah was Israel's *problem*. Hence faithfully keeping Torah was Israel's *solution* for ushering in the age of the messiah.

Which brings us to Paul's dilemma.

If Torah-breaking was in fact Israel's problem that kept the Jews from being fully delivered and restored, how in the world can an executed and raised messiah be God's solution? That makes no sense.

Unless, maybe, Torah-breaking isn't really *the* problem.

If Jesus dying and walking out of a tomb is God's *solution,* maybe the problem—the deeper problem—God has in his sights is . . . *death.*

Death is (last time I looked) a universal problem, not just a Jewish one. So defeating death is a solution for everyone.

Likewise, sin—disobedience to God and unjust actions toward others—was also a universal problem. Jesus's death was not simply another Roman execution, but sacrifice for sins—not just for Jews, but Gentiles, too.

Sin was *everybody's* problem, and sin went deeper than whether or not Jews kept Torah. Sin gets right to the core of the *human* predicament. All humans are in the same boat, and it's sinking.

That's a lot to take in, but welcome to the world of the apostle Paul: he's a complicated guy. And we're not quite done. We are coming now to a key part of Paul's thinking.

Since the problem (sin and death) and the solution (Jesus's death and resurrection) apply equally to Jews and Gentiles, it stands to reason that there can only be *one people of God,* made up of Jews and Gentiles, who benefit equally from what God has done.

That does not mean Jews (or Gentiles) lost their ethnicity or culture. It means, though, that both have *full and equal* access to God *as they are.* That access is through faith in Christ, obedience to *him,* rather than through Torah-keeping.

Paul understood how new this idea would sound to others. He calls it a "mystery" that wasn't known before this time, but is now revealed by God's spirit: "The Gentiles have become fellow heirs [with the Jews], members of the same body, and sharers in the promise in Christ Jesus through the Gospel."

We should linger here for a moment, for it summarizes a main theme of Paul's letters: God's unexpected move—Jesus's death and resurrection—places Jews *and* Gentiles on *equal footing* with God. As Paul writes, "there is no distinction between Jew and Greek." The "wall of hostility" between them has been torn down. No hierarchy, no barriers, no us versus them.

That idea didn't catch on at first. Peter, one of Jesus's disciples, whose stubbornness rivaled Paul's own, had issues with it.

You can't blame him. His scripture—the same Bible Paul read—seemed to be pretty clear about some barriers at least between God's Chosen People and everyone else. In Peter and Paul's day, Gentiles could worship Israel's God and follow the basic ethics of Judaism ("God fearers" as they were called). But now, Paul argued, Jesus made it so that Gentiles were true equals, with no need to follow Jewish tradition to worship the Jewish God, and with neither Jew nor Gentile as first-class members. We can put ourselves in Peter's place and see his point.

Explaining how the Jesus story made Israel's story an every-person story is more or less what Paul's letters are about, not every word or verse, but the heart of them. And to pull that off—namely, to convince his fellow Jewish Christians—*Paul had to present Israel's story as a universal story.*

Paul transforms a tribal story, of kings, land, and the purity of one group of people, into a global story of God's grace and peace to all nations. As famously confusing as Paul's letters are, if we keep this in mind, a lot of what Paul says will make more sense—such as the following.

"Torah? Oh That. It Was Only Temporary."

—God (As Told to Paul)

TORAH WAS THE CENTERPIECE of Israel's communion with God. It was commanded by God through Moses and, according to Israel's story, had no expiration date. The people of God were bound by God himself to keep Torah. End of discussion.

Then Paul comes on the scene and contends that Jesus made Gentiles every bit as much members of the people of God as Israelites had always been. So here's the issue that came up almost instantly: since Gentiles are now welcome as full members in Israel's story, does that mean they also need to keep the Torah, seeing that Torah had no expiration date and was commanded by God himself?

In other words, did Gentiles have to convert, as it were, to Judaism, in order to be followers of the Jewish messiah? Paul answered "no."

And not only was that a big fat no for Gentiles, but for Jews too.

Since Jewish and Gentile followers of Jesus are now equal members of the family of God and therefore *one people,* Paul argues that Jesus put an end to the *requirement* of Torah-keeping not only for Gentiles but also for Jews. That means Torah takes a backseat to Jesus—for Jews and Gentiles.

That doesn't mean Jewish followers of Jesus *had* to stop getting circumcised, for example, or refraining from eating pork.

It means, though, that faithfulness to God would no longer be defined by Torah-keeping.

Talk about rewriting Israel's story around Jesus.

Some Jewish followers of Jesus were understandably upset with Paul—and it's not hard to put ourselves in their place and see why. Even though Jesus was a surprise ending, Jewish followers of Jesus did not for one moment think that meant abandoning tradition and starting a new religion. Their Jewish identity remained fully intact and they naturally assumed that the Torah that God himself put into place long ago still applied with full force.

Paul would agree, to a certain extent. He did not think that Jesus was the founder of a new religion, rather the concluding, chapter to Israel's story. Paul was clearly on board with that idea 100 percent—in fact he spends much of his letters making that case.

On the other hand, key elements of Israel's story, which had been sacred to Jewish identity for a thousand years, were deemed by Paul null and void.

Not always known for his calming manner, in one place, no doubt in the heat of debate, Paul calls some of the old ways "rubbish" in order to "gain Christ." Elsewhere, he says that God has "abolished the law with its commandments and ordinances, that he might create in himself one new humanity in the place of two [Jew and Gentile]."

We should feel free to see a tension in Paul's thinking, a paradox as I mentioned earlier: what God has done in Jesus is deeply connected to Israel's story while at the same time breaking out of the confines of that story. As soon as we try to resolve that paradox in Paul we will misunderstand him.

And there's more.

Paul not only argues that Torah-keeping is *no longer* central for Israel's God. He argues in a few places that in God's mind *it never really was*—a definite double-take moment for anyone, if you're following along in Israel's story. Reading the Old Testament on its own terms would never lead anyone to conclude that Torah was anything other than front and center in God's plans.

But Paul isn't reading the Old Testament on its own terms. Paul rereads his Bible through the lens of Jesus, God's final word.

That final word is Paul's nonnegotiable *starting and ending point* for understanding Israel's story. The reality of Jesus as crucified and risen messiah obligates Paul to rethink—even overturn in places—his Bible.

If there is any cure for thinking of the Bible as a once-told-forever-binding source of information about God and his people, Paul is it.

For example, Paul argues that the story of Abraham reveals that, despite appearances, law-keeping was never God's main focus. Mind you, Abraham was the *father of all Israel*. What in the world is Paul up to?

Paul's got a bit of a point. In the book of Romans, he reminds his readers that God called Abraham from his homeland and made a pact with him long before God actually gave the law to Moses several hundred years later on Mount Sinai.

Hence, Paul reasons, if God began his relationship with his people apart from Torah-keeping, then Torah-keeping doesn't secure anyone's status before God. Only faithfulness to God does, *the very kind of faithfulness that Abraham showed* when he trusted God enough to leave his homeland, trek down to Canaan, and to accept God's promise to give him and his wife, Sarah, a child (Isaac) in their old age. Things like sacrifices and purity laws weren't in the picture yet.

Paul got creative with a verse in the Abraham story to "prove" that faith in God, not Torah-keeping, was the key for God. God promised that Abraham's descendants would be as numerous as the stars of heaven. We read that Abraham "believed the Lord" and in return the Lord counted that belief as "righteousness" on Abraham's part. Long before there ever was Torah, Paul argues, Abraham's "belief" (better "trust") in God made him "righteous" in God's eyes. Hence, Paul argues, faith makes us right with God, not Torah.

I'd pay good money to know how the Jewish Christians in Rome would have reacted to this bit of creative reading of the Abraham story. If you look at that one verse in context in Genesis, all it says is that God commends Abraham for his trust in the promise.

But Paul sees this one verse as overturning what is rather obvious and pervasive throughout the Old Testament: Torah is a huge deal in how God and Israel relate to each other.

Later in Romans, Paul goes even further: Torah only entered the drama later on in order *to expose* the depth of human sinfulness. The Old Testament never puts it that way, though. Torah is given to Israel as part of the "covenant" (agreement) between God and Israel.

And Torah was not a burden, but a light for one's walk with God, a way to keep from stumbling, a gift from God to his people. And as we've seen Israel was expected to keep Torah—they were blessed if they did but punished if they didn't.

Paul is arguing that Torah is not the true center of what God has been up to all these years. Paul decenters Torah for his Jewish readers, treating it almost as an afterthought, and replaces it with a new center to God's story: Jesus. And Paul uses the Abraham story to make his point.

Paul hits this idea from another angle in the book of Galatians. He argues that Torah was only a *temporary* move on God's part. He compares Torah to a "guardian" of small children—designed to keep "minors" in line as "slaves" are kept in line by their master. So Torah is not a mark of true freedom and spiritual maturity as in the Old Testament. It is a slave master, a nanny for small children (Old Testament Israel) until Jesus came to do away with all that.

Paul isn't done. A few verses later in Galatians, he presents a creative reading of Abraham's wife Sarah and her Egyptian slave woman Hagar. Paul says that Torah and Mount Sinai are a kind of slavery, represented by Hagar. The son born to her, Abraham's first son, Ishmael, was therefore born into a state of slavery.

To be clear, Paul is saying that the slave woman Hagar and her slave child Ishmael illustrate *Torah*.

Sarah, on the other hand, is a free woman and bears Isaac, a son of promise, born into freedom. For Paul, Sarah and Isaac represent what God is doing now in light of Jesus, freeing Jews and Gentiles from the burden of submitting to the "slavish" demands of the law.

Let that sink in.

The story of Sarah, the wife of *Abraham,* ancient mother of all Israel, demonstrates in Paul's mind that Torah-keeping is slavery. He doesn't tie Sarah to God's gift of the law and the entire story of Israel, as any normal reader of the Old Testament would do. He ties Torah to Hagar, Sarah's *slave*—and an Egyptian one at that.

Paul's description of the value of Torah doesn't seem very Jewish—and with that I gladly accept the committee's nomination for the "Understatement of the Year" award (which I assume carries with it a cash prize of some sort).

To sum up: Paul says Torah was never central to God but only temporary, a placeholder playing a supporting role until Jesus came to replace it. Any normal Jew, hearing Paul describe Israel's faith this way, would have thought he was having a nervous breakdown. Imagine today walking into your average church one Sunday and hearing a pastor say that there's been a change in plans, and now the true way of following Jesus is to sing the praises of Allah and his one prophet, Mohammed. An emergency pastoral search committee would be convened before the closing hymn.

Paul transforms Israel's story from a Torah-centered faith of one small ethnic group to a universal story that decentered Torah and put the crucified and resurrected Jesus in its place. Despite the surprise factor, Paul argues, what God is doing now in Jesus, not Torah, was *God's plan all along.*

What we have here is a radical rethinking—actually, a rewriting—of Israel's story, driven by Paul's faith in Jesus as God's Son, the surprise ending to Israel's story.

To see what Paul sees, Christians today are summoned to join Paul: the reality of Jesus demands that the Old Testament be read not by the book, but against the grain.

Which brings us to penises and ham sandwiches.

"Why Don't You Just Go Castrate Yourself," and Other Spiritual Advice

AS I'VE BEEN SAYING, following Torah was an understandably central issue for Jews in Paul's day. Surrounded by Romans, Jews were careful to maintain Torah, especially those laws that would clearly mark them off from their Roman landlords.

Two of these laws were circumcision and dietary restrictions. These "boundary markers" were visible, concrete ways that Jews could show their allegiance to God, proof that they hadn't caved in to Roman ways. Like wearing a WWJD bracelet and drinking club soda at a frat party, some behaviors clearly mark you off as belonging to a different crowd.

Paul zeroed in on these boundary markers and told Jewish and Gentile Christians that they were no longer valid as boundary markers. In fact, claiming that they *were* got in the way of true faith in God—even though God was the one who wrote these regulations in stone centuries earlier.

Now the only marker that counts, the marker that truly designates you as someone who serves Israel's God and not Roman gods, is "faith [in Christ] working through love"—faith in Jesus demonstrated in how you treat others.

The problem, of course, was that circumcision wasn't voluntary. God declared to Abraham all males of Israel be circumcised on the eighth day. This ritual was to be an "everlasting" sign that distinguished the Israelites as Yahweh's people. Whoever did not comply with cutting off the foreskin of the penis was himself "cut off" from his people—which probably meant excommunicated, but the pun certainly gets your attention.

Even though the Old Testament never explicitly says "Gentiles must be circumcised to convert" (although the original command in Genesis does say that foreign slaves are included), we can't blame the Jewish followers of Jesus if they assumed that this unexpected Gentile influx would need to be brought under the Old Testament umbrella. Gentiles would have to show their allegiance to Israel's God in the same way as Jews always have, in the way that God had commanded long ago.

Paul responds by lobbing hand grenades on his own Jewish tradition: those who insist that circumcision is still required are *distorting* God's will. Those who insist on continuing to follow God's command from of old are actually opposing God for failing to recognize that the crucified and resurrected Jesus is the final word of God to his people and overturns the "works of the law."

And—as if to drive the point home—Paul suggests that those who are so uptight about circumcision should do everyone a favor and castrate themselves while they are at it. And if that doesn't make you want to sit down and read every square inch of Paul's letters, nothing will.

What drove Paul to handle circumcision like this? Was he just sitting around reading his Bible, minding his own business, and it popped into his head, *Hey, I think I'll undermine the Bible*? No.

Paul's commitment to the resurrected Jesus as God's final word drove him to rethink and transform his tradition and his scripture. Because of Jesus, the physical marker commanded by God to be an everlasting command to mark off the people of God had met its expiration date.

Getting Jesus right dictated how Paul reread his Bible—and in this case, rereading Israel's story meant erasing part of it.

The same principle holds for food restrictions, the list of "clean" and "unclean" foods God gave to Moses.

Eating—even touching—unclean foods made Israelites and the clothes on their backs unclean for the rest of the day. That might not sound like the end of the world to us: eat some pork and become "unclean" for a few hours, wait for the sun to go down, and we're good. But it was a big deal for ancient Israelites, and judging by Paul's letter to the Romans, it was also a big deal for Jews living under the Romans.

Not only was the temptation to eat like Romans an issue, but simply touching unclean food could happen at any moment, even by accident. You sit down where some Roman had just polished off some pork, and if you touch a molecule of it, you are technically unclean.

Paul had no intention whatsoever of leaving this alone.

In the book of Romans, Paul works hard to convince his readers of a mixed Jewish/Gentile congregation that they need to lay down their ancient hostilities and act like one people. Jews were on the scene first, and so they felt they ranked higher than these newbie Gentiles. Gentiles, since they didn't have all that food regulation business to attend to, snickered a bit at the old-fashioned, backwater Jews.

But, if the gospel means anything, Paul argues, the people of God should not act this way toward each other. So here is Paul's solution: he tells those who are "strong" to put up with those who are "weak" and not make their lives difficult.

Paul's not talking about hitting the weight room or carrying groceries for the elderly. Although he never spells it out, it's clear enough that the "weak" are those who still feel they need to keep the commands of God to eat kosher. The "strong" are those who know that, because of Jesus, they can live free of those commands.

Paul pushes this a step further. If you really want to be shown to be a follower of Jesus, the strong, even though they are right, shouldn't rub their freedom in the faces of their weaker brothers and sisters by sitting down next to them and eating lobster bisque. Sure, they *can*—in the sense that God is just fine with lobster now—but they *shouldn't* if in doing so they will undermine the faith of their weaker brother or sister.

There is no higher "law" to be obeyed than the law of love. That, at the end of the day, is what it means to follow Jesus.

Jesus brings freedom, but even more he brings a new vision of self-sacrificial love, even—especially—among two people groups with a long history of tension, if not out-and-out hostility toward each other.

For Paul, Jesus—crucified and risen from the dead—is how God had surprisingly shown up for "his people," meaning everyone, just as they are, from every nation, all on equal footing. Paul explained God's surprising move by rereading Israel's story with Jesus at the center.

*   *   *

In principle, what Paul does here is no different from what we've seen in chapter 3: the present shapes how you think about the past. This was true of those who told the stories of Israel's past—the realities of Israel's monarchy and then exile shaped how Israel's storytellers talked about their past.

Paul's "present" is the surprising, dramatic upheaval of Jesus, and so he reshapes Israel's past more dramatically and radically.

Sticking to the Bible at every turn, like it's an owner's manual or book of instruction, as the way to know God misses what Paul and the rest of the New Testament writers show us again and again: the words on the page of the Bible don't drive the story, Jesus does. Jesus is bigger than the Bible.

For Christians, then, the question is not "Who gets the Bible right?" The question is and has always been, "Who gets Jesus right?" The Gospel writers and Paul couldn't have made that any clearer.

Chapter
Seven

The Bible, Just as It Is

For Those on the Go, the Entire Book in Exactly 265 Words
(With Brief Commentary)

The Bible is an ancient book and we shouldn't be surprised to see it act like one. So seeing God portrayed as a violent, tribal warrior is not how God is but how he was understood to be by the ancient Israelites communing with God in their time and place.

The biblical writers were storytellers. Writing about the past was never simply about understanding the past for its own sake, but about shaping, molding, and creating the past to speak to the present. "Getting the past right" wasn't the driving issue. "Who are we now?" was.

The Bible presents a variety of points of view about God and what it means to walk in his ways. This stands to reason, since the biblical writers lived at different times, in different places, and wrote for different reasons. In reading the Bible we are watching the spiritual journeys of people long ago.

Jesus, like other Jews of the first century, read his Bible creatively, seeking deeper meaning that transcended or simply bypassed the boundaries of the words of scripture. Where Jesus ran afoul of the official interpreters of the Bible of his day was not in his creative handling of the Bible, but in drawing attention to his own authority and status in doing so.

A crucified and resurrected messiah was a surprise ending to Israel's story. To spread the word of this messiah, the earliest Christian writers both respected Israel's story while also going beyond that story. They transformed it from a story of Israel centered on Torah to a story of humanity centered on Jesus.

This is the Bible we have, the Bible where God meets us.

Not a book kept at a safe distance from the human drama. Not a fragile Bible that has to be handled with care lest it crumble in our hands. Not a book that has to be defended 24/7 to make sure our faith doesn't dissolve.

In other words, not an artificially well-behaved Bible that gives false comfort, but the Holy Bible, the Word of God, with wrinkles, complexities, unexpected maneuvers, and downright strangeness.

This is the Bible God has given his people. *This* Bible is worth reading and paying attention to, because this is the Bible God uses, as he always has, to point its readers to a deeper trust in him.

We are free to walk away from this invitation, of course, but we are not free to make a Bible in our own image. What the Bible looks like is God's call, not ours.

A Quick Thought About the Universe and God Laughing

SOME VERY SMART PEOPLE with large telescopes and math skills tell us that the (known) universe is about 13.7 billion years old. Traveling at the speed of light (approximately 186,000 miles per second = 37 round-trip flights per second between New York and Los Angeles), it would take about 100 billion years to get from one end of the universe to the other.

Light travels about 5.87 trillion miles a year. When I tell my calculator to multiply that number by 100 billion years to get the approximate total number of miles across the universe, it gives me the following: 5.87E23.

I think my calculator blew a gasket or something. When calculators start using letters, it's best just to walk away. After an extensive Google search I learned that my calculator is trying to say 587 sextillion (587,000,000,000,000,000,000,000). I think we all agree that this number is incomprehensible.

This is what God laughing looks like. It also makes me wonder why I would ever try to write a book about God, though I probably should have thought about that two hundred pages ago.

Moving along, this unimaginably large universe contains perhaps as many as one trillion galaxies, thousands of light-years apart, each containing billions and billions of stars also light-years apart.

If that's not enough to take in, we are also told that the universe apparently doesn't feel it's big enough yet; it is expanding, whatever that means. And now some are even saying there may be more than one.

At the other end of the scale we have atoms, which are too small to think about (1/10,000,000 of a millimeter). And just to be annoying, there are subatomic particles.

Or just take the earth, something we can picture, a mere 4.5 billion years young. If the age of the earth were scaled to the length of a football field, my life and yours would be about 4/100,000 of an inch from the goal line; a sheet of paper is one hundred times thicker. If the age of the earth were scaled to a calendar year, our lives would be about the last three-tenths of a second before New Year's Day. Jesus lived at 11:59 and 47.4 seconds P.M.

To sum up: the universe is beyond comprehension.

Christians believe that God, the one responsible for the incomprehensible—in a further incomprehensible move—entered into the human drama.

So, right off the bat, I'm going with *mystery* as an operative category for talking about God.

And I expect to be surprised by this God.

Which brings me to the Bible.

The Bible was written by a small band of people in one small part of one planet in one galaxy over a minuscule one-thousand-year period. This Bible carries the thoughts and meditations of ancient pilgrims and, I believe, according to God's purpose, has guided, comforted, and informed Christians for as long as there have been Christians.

But this God of the unintelligibly huge, immeasurably small, and incomprehensibly old creation is not fully captured or constrained by those words. He can't be. And we don't need astrophysics or electron microscopes to tell us that. The Holy Bible does that already.

Whenever we think we have God in a box, safe and sound, under control and constant watch, God blows up our categories.

That is the lesson we learn from the Old Testament, Israel's story. God meets the ancient Israelites as they are able to understand him—as a warrior who slays his enemies, human and divine; a deity who is appeased by the blood of animals; a God who commands that eating lobster and bodily discharges make one "unclean," and considers virgin daughters spoils of war and the property of their fathers.

And just when it seems this is all there is to say, God also meets the Israelites in unexpected ways, in crisis, in exile, and he is on the move, challenging his people not to limit his actions by their perceptions. On the pages of the Old Testament we see the ancient sages and storytellers pondering a God who won't sit still long enough to have the cement of people's perceptions dry around him.

And then in the Gospels and letters of the New Testament, God bursts on the scene again, at first in an expected way using the familiar language of messiah, kingdom, and liberation. But just when even Jesus's closest followers thought they knew God's next move, God acts with unnerving freedom: death and resurrection, with equal access to God for all.

I think part of what it means for God to "reveal" himself is to keep us guessing, to come to terms with the idea that knowing God is also a form of not knowing God, of knowing that we cannot fully know, but only catch God in part—which is more than enough to keep us busy.

If we read the Bible today thinking that this God of creation, freedom, and mystery is bound by a book as if it were a contract, with nothing left to say, no further moves or surprises, we will miss much. The Bible tells us so.

Not That I'm Trying to Tell You What to Do, But . . .

THIS BOOK is really about having an attitude adjustment concerning the Bible and God in light of how the Bible actually behaves. That's the idea, at least, and here are some big thoughts I try to keep in mind as I continue to work all this out for myself.

* * *

The Bible is God's Word. The Bible has been around a long time and it's not going anywhere. Even with all its challenges and odd stories, its naysayers and skeptics, it's got staying power. People just keep right along meeting God there.

Forget everything else. Forget all the reasons we might have for putting it away in a box somewhere with other ancient relics. Forget the fact that God often has a temper and commands strange things. Forget the fact that its writers thought the earth was flat, a flood covered the earth, or the first woman held a conversation with a snake.

The Bible, just as it is, still works.

Don't try to explain it. Just accept it. That won't make you a mindless zombie. It just means you are accepting your own human limitations and acknowledging by faith that something bigger than ourselves is happening, someone bigger is behind it, and we have the privilege to be a part of it.

Hold on to the time-tested wisdom that in order to know God better, we should keep reading and wrestling with the Bible. It's God's Word and that's what he wants.

*   *   *

The Bible is not, never has been, and never will be the center of the Christian faith. Even though the Bible (at least in some form) has been ever present since the beginning of Christianity, it's not the central focus of the Christian faith. That position belongs to God, specifically, what God has done in and through Jesus. The Bible is the church's nonnegotiable partner, but it is not God's final word: Jesus is.

Of course, the Bible is what tells us about this Jesus, but that doesn't put the Bible in the center. As theologians tell us, the Bible, in various and complex ways, "bears witness" to Christ. That is the Bible's role, to encourage the faithful to live in its pages *in order to* look up from the pages and, by the power and love of the Spirit of God, see Jesus.

The Bible doesn't say, "Look at me!" It says, "Look through me." The Bible, if we are paying attention, decenters itself.

*   *   *

The Bible is not a weapon. We read in the book of Hebrews that,

> . . . the word of God is living and active, sharper than any two-edged sword, piercing until it divides soul from spirit, joints from marrow; it is able to judge the thoughts and intentions of the heart.

If I had a dollar for every time I've heard that passage misused I could afford my own sports franchise—at least the Chicago Cubs.

The Bible isn't a lightsaber for lopping off the heads of people we disagree with. For one thing, "word of God" here in Hebrews doesn't mean "the Bible" but God speaking in fresh ways by what he was doing through Jesus. If you look just before this passage, the author of Hebrews goes through a lengthy *creative* interpretation of Psalm 95, giving it *new* meaning in light of the new thing God is doing among them centered on Jesus.

More important, the word of God as a two-edged sword is supposed to be turned inward, piercing us, not everyone around us. You don't wield the sword. God does. God doesn't call people to do that, and thinking that he does is a sign of our own insecurities.

The Bible is not a weapon, a sword to be wielded today against modern-day Canaanites or Babylonians. It is a book where we meet God. It brings hope, encouragement, knowledge, and deep truth for those willing to risk, to "die" to themselves, as Jesus puts it, to accept the challenge of scripture, knowing they will be undone in the process.

That journey is lifelong, marked by discipline and humility, to know the Bible intimately, with agility and gentleness—an arena of spiritual growth, for love of God and humanity, not for World Bible Extreme Cagefighting.

And yes, in the history of Christianity, there have been times of needed debate and drawing lines. But (1) we should hate to have to do that rather than salivating at the thought, (2) we shouldn't be nasty, and (3) we should be extra clear the issue at hand is worth fighting for.

But looking for fights—encouraging and even creating controversy thinking that God wills it—is pathological.

*   *   *

An unsettled faith is a maturing faith. Christians often get the signal from others that if they doubt or struggle in some way with the Bible, their faith is weak. They are told that their goal should be to ease the stress somehow by praying more, going to church twice on Sunday (and Wednesday if need be), or generally just stop being so rebelliously stubborn and asking so many questions.

But one thing we see in the Bible is how often people's trust in God was shaken—and not because they were weak, but because life happens. Whether we read books like Job and Ecclesiastes (as we've seen) or the dozens of psalms that cry out to God for some reason or another, life does not move along smoothly.

You get the feeling from the Bible that being unsettled is almost a normal part of the process.

Not that we should go looking for it—it will find us soon enough—but struggling in some way seems like something we should expect on our own spiritual journeys. True struggling in faith is a stretching experience, and without it, you don't mature in your faith. You either remain an infant or get cocky.

Feeling dis-ease and challenged in faith may be God pushing us out of our own safety zone, where we rest on our own ideas about God and confuse those ideas with the real thing. God may be pushing us to experience him more fully, with us kicking and screaming all the way if need be.

Feeling unsettled may be God telling us lovingly, but still in his typical attention-getting manner, it's time to grow.

*   *   *

Let go of fear. If I had to name the most common obstacle for Christians to a life of true trust in God, it would be fear—mainly the fear of being wrong about the Bible, which is often equated with being wrong about God.

What we believe about God is very important to us, as it should be. Our faith defines who we are and helps us make sense of the world around us and the world that awaits us afterward. Our faith is the page upon which our personal narratives are written. To feel that our faith is threatened can easily turn to fear.

But, judging from the long and varied history of thinking within Christianity, "being right" is elusive, and the Bible is never something we will actually master. The relentless and sinful human habit of creating God to look like ourselves, and thus distorting God, is also a constant problem.

The choice we all need to make daily is whether we are willing to hold our narratives with an open hand and let God rewrite them when necessary.

In the spiritual life, the opposite of fear is not courage, but trust.

*   *   *

Branch out. Not only do our beliefs define us, but so does the community of like-minded people who share those beliefs. Christian traditions, denominations, and congregations provide a group identity.

We are social animals, so we should not judge our spiritual groups, or those of others, as necessarily a problem. Only when our communities become *the* defining element of our spiritual lives, packs that protect those boundaries at all costs, do problems begin. That leads to isolation, "us versus them" thinking, and the illusion that "we" are basically right about the Bible and God and "they" aren't—the kind of wall-building that Jesus and Paul criticized.

So much can be learned from other traditions. In the long history of the Christian church, so many different, even conflicting, points of view have been embraced as true and valuable. Even today, at this very moment, literally thousands of recognized, established, Christian denominations dot the world, where members worship God and understand his ways differently from each other.

Some think the presence of diversity in the church is a problem that needs correcting: "they" haven't gotten the memo yet that "we" are right, and as soon as "they" fall into line, God's will will finally be done on earth as it is in heaven, amen.

For any one group today to think it has the best grasp on the creator of the universe is a form of insanity. Run away—far and quickly—when you see this.

The presence of diverse points of view in the church is unavoidable, seeing that—as we saw in chapter 4—people of faith, including those we read about in the Bible, are always meeting God where they are, asking their questions within their contexts.

Who we are always affects our spiritual perceptions. Maybe God likes the diversity. If he doesn't, we'd have to conclude that he hasn't done a good job of controlling it. But maybe diversity tells us something about what God is like.

All this is to say, if your present community sees your spiritual journey as a problem because you are wandering off their beach blanket, it may be time to find another community. One should never do that impulsively. But if after a time you are sensing that you do not belong, that you are a problem to be corrected rather than a valued member of the community, maybe God is calling you elsewhere and to find for yourself that "they" aren't so bad after all.

That decision is very personal (sometimes involving whole families) and can take some courage to make, but it is worth the risk. One thing is certain: if you stay where you are without any change at all, the pressure to either conform or keep quiet will work in you like a slow-acting poison.

And if you go too far down that road, it can be a tough haul coming back from bitterness and resentment—especially for children.

*   *   *

Take a page or two out of Judaism. A famous story from the Talmud, Judaism's early medieval core text on Jewish faith and life, records a debate between rabbis. The debate is over whether an oven that was made impure could be purified and used again.

The majority opinion was no but one rabbi, Eliezar, argued the opposite, but, alas, to no avail. Exasperated by his colleagues' dim-wittedness, he challenged them with some miracles. If I am right, he said, may that tree over there move—whereupon the tree picked itself up and moved about the length of a football field. But the others weren't convinced. They were certain their argument from the Bible was sure, and no moving tree was going to convince them otherwise.

Eliezar wouldn't give up. He called a stream to reverse course and then the walls of the house to bend inward, but the others responded the same way. Finally, Eliezar asked whether hearing the heavenly voice of God himself would convince them, at which point the voice of God declared that Eliezar was absolutely right.

This didn't work either. The others responded that God had already given his Torah on Mount Sinai. In that Torah we read that God's commands are "not in heaven" but right here, available to all. God himself is bound by his own recorded words in Torah, and so even his heavenly voice can't change that.

At hearing this, God laughed with delight, "My children have defeated me! My children have defeated me!"

This story illustrates something Judaism seems to have a good handle on but that many Christians do not: debating each other, and debating God, is what God wants.

We can see the same sort of attitude in the rich tradition of Jewish medieval commentaries on the Bible. The sages of Judaism debate the meaning of biblical passages, often arriving at contradictory explanations—and all of it is recorded and preserved as part of the sacred tradition, without any need to resolve the problem and arrive at a final answer.

Even in their debates, though, we see their affirmations: God exists; he has given us his law; it is important that we wrestle with it and make sure we honor God in how we keep his law—even if we disagree. But killing the possibility of debate is what kills the faith. The debate keeps the *conversation* at the center of the community.

Ending the debate, getting to the right answer, is not the prime directive in the spiritual life. You can tussle with each other and with God (and win!), and it's all good. The back-and-forth with the Bible *is* where God is found. Enter the dialogue and you find God waiting for you, laughing with delight, ready to be a part of that back-and-forth.

*   *   *

Christian, don't expect more from the Bible than you would of Jesus. The grand mystery of the Christian faith is that God has entered the human drama. God incarnate—literally "in-fleshed," as the theologians say.

This Jesus was born of a Jewish woman in first-century Galilee. Like everyone else, he grew from an infant to adult. He learned how to speak the local languages, how to read and write, how to tie his sandals, and eventually learned a trade, carpentry.

He learned through his parents and good old trial and error the ways of his culture and the subtle social rules that never make it into any history book. He figured things out and made mistakes along the way. He would feel frustrated, angry, happy, relieved, sorry, ashamed, surprised, happy, sad.

Jesus, in other words, was not an alien, nor was he God simply dressed up as a human being. He *was,* as the Christian theologians have always said, human through and through, and a particular kind of human (as Christian theologians sometimes forget): a Jewish male living in the Roman world of first-century Judea.

If you saw Jesus walking down the street back then, you wouldn't notice anything all that special—no glow around his head or lightning bolts shooting out of his eye. And, like the rest of us, he had periods of suffering and then eventually died.

That is how Christians believe God showed up—in-fleshed in humility, in culture, in the human story, a peasant who fit right into the day-to-day world of the first century and then suffered the humiliation of execution. No entourage, no special treatment, no red carpet, no clout among the power brokers.

If Christians are right and this is the ultimate way God showed up, we shouldn't expect anything else from the Bible.

A well-behaved Bible is one that rises above the messy and inconvenient ups and downs of life. A Bible like that is an alien among its surroundings, a brittle scroll kept under glass, safe and sound from the rough handling of the outside world.

Such a Bible is nothing like Jesus. It also doesn't exist.

The Bible looks the way it does because, like Jesus, when God shows up, it's in the thick of things—as Matthew's Gospel says, Immanuel, God *with* us. This is the paradox, the mystery, and the Good News of the Christian faith.

If we let the Bible be the Bible, on its own terms—on God's terms—we will see this in-fleshing God at work, not despite the challenges, the unevenness, and ancient strangeness of the Bible, but precisely *because* of these things. Perhaps not the way we would have written our sacred book, if we had been consulted, but the one that the good and wise God has allowed his people to have.

If we come to the Bible and read it this way, in true humility, rather than defending our version of it, we will find God as he wants to be found.

The Bible tells us so.

Where in the Bible Were We?
(In Order of Appearance)

CHAPTER 1—I'LL TAKE DOOR NUMBER THREE

Concerning Camels' Backs and Beach Balls. The "movable rock" tradition is in 1 Corinthians 10:4. The Old Testament passages that refer to the miraculous supply of water from a rock are Exodus 17:1–7 (at the beginning of the forty years in the wilderness) and Numbers 20:1–13 (at the end).

CHAPTER 2—GOD DID *WHAT*?!

How Not to Treat Other People. The biblical passages I allude to for God's violence are Genesis 6–7; 22:1–19; Exodus 12:29–32; 14:26–31 (also 15:1–19); Exodus 32; Leviticus 10:1–3. The biblical laws that carry the death penalty are in Deuteronomy 13:6–11; Leviticus 20:10, 24:10–23, and Exodus 31:12–17.

Those Wicked, Horrible Canaanites. The flood story is found in Genesis 6–9, and the part about Ham's sin and the curse of his son Canaan is in 9:18–29. The other passages in Genesis that refer to Canaan are 12:6 and 15:12–16 (residents of Canaan are called "Amorites").

Marching Orders. The Israelites' stay at Mount Sinai begins at Exodus 19 and continues through Leviticus to Numbers 10 (eleven months in all), at which point they break camp and head to Canaan. The spies are sent out in Numbers 13–14, and the "marching orders" for the conquest are given in Deuteronomy 20:10–20 (but also look at verses 1–9 to get a fuller picture).

The book of Joshua records the conquest itself. The stories of Jericho and Ai are in chapters 6–8, the Gibeonite incident is in chapter 9, and the battle against the "five kings" is in 10:16–43. The list of thirty-one Canaanite towns under Israelite control is in 12:7–24, and the story of the towns conquered before the Israelites crossed the Jordan (on the way into Canaan) is in Numbers 21:21–35.

The incomplete purge of the Canaanites is mentioned in the book of Judges, and God's purposes for letting them remain are found in Judges 2:20–3:1.

"If Jesus Sends People to Hell, What's So Bad About Killing Some Canaanites??" The references to *Gehenna* in the Gospels are Matthew 5:22, 29, 30; 10:28; 18:9; 23:15, 33; Mark 9:43, 45, 47; Luke 12:5. Jeremiah mentions the "Valley of Hinnom" in Jeremiah 7:30–8:3 and 19:4–9 (see also Joshua 15:8). The reference to fire is in Isaiah 66:24.

The "Canaanite" woman in Matthew is found in 15:21–28 (Mark's version is in 7:24–30). My source for this insight is Kenton L. Sparks, "Gospel as Conquest: Mosaic Typology in Matthew 28:16–20," *Catholic Biblical Quarterly* 68 (2006): 651–63.

Jesus's responses to violent political takeover are taken from John 18:36 and Matthew 5:5, 9, and 44–45 (Sermon on the Mount). A passage in the Old Testament prophets that anticipates Jesus's view of God's people influencing the world around them positively rather than waging war is Isaiah 58:10.

God's Nicer Side. References to God's compassion and being slow to anger toward the Israelites are Exodus 34:6 and Ezekiel 18:23. These words are also used with respect to the Ninevites in Jonah 4:2–3. The story of God's compassion on Rahab from Jericho is in Joshua 6.

Worst. Sinners. Ever. The gross immorality of the Canaanites is outlined in Leviticus 18. King Mesha's sacrifice of his son is in 2 Kings 3:4–27. The other incidents of child sacrifice in the Bible I mention are Genesis 22:1–19 (Isaac) and Judges 11 (Jephthah's daughter).

The incident involving the Moabites and taking captive virgin woman is in Numbers 31 (and see chapter 25 for the background). The statistics for genocide in the twentieth century are from http://en.wikipedia.org/wiki/List_of_genocides_by_death_toll.

Digging for Answers. The archaeological overview concerning the thirty-one towns in Israel (and four towns on the other side of the Jordan River—Heshbon, Sihon, Medeba, and Dibon [see Numbers 21:21–31]) follows Douglas A. Knight and Amy-Jill Levine, *The Meaning of the Bible: What the Jewish Scriptures and Christian Old Testament Can Teach Us* (HarperOne, 2011), 20–21. Also Lawrence E. Stager, "Forging and Identity: The Emergence of Ancient Israel," 123–75, in *The Oxford History of the Biblical World,* ed. Michael D. Coogan (OUP, 1998).

Why This Chapter Is So Important and So Dreadfully Long. The reference to the 200-mile-long river of blood is from Revelation 14:17–20. The talking animals are found in Genesis 3:1–7 (serpent) and Numbers 22:22–40 (donkey). The Ten Commandments are found in Exodus 20:2–17 and (a different version) Deuteronomy 5:6–21. The law concerning virgin daughters as property is found in Exodus 22:16–17, dietary laws in Leviticus 11, and the stoning of the rebellious son in Deuteronomy 21:18–21. One of many references to "Sheol" (the abode of the dead) is Psalm 6:5.

CHAPTER 3—GOD LIKES STORIES

The Stories of Jesus. The scene with Jesus turning over tables in the temple is found in Matthew 21:12–17, Mark 11:15–19, Luke 19:45–48, and John 2:13–25.

Little Baby Jesuses. The birth stories are found in Matthew 1:18–2:23 and Luke 1:5–2:40. Matthew's exodus allusions are from Exodus 13:17–22 (pillar of fire) and 1:22 (drowning of male infants). The song of Hannah, which is mirrored in Mary's song of praise, is found in 1 Samuel 2:1–10.

Who Saw the Big Moment? The resurrection accounts are in Matthew 27:62–28:20, Mark 16:1–8 (shorter ending) and 16:9–20 (longer ending), Luke 24, and John 20–21. Jesus's response to "Doubting Thomas's" confession is in John 20:29.

The Stories of Israel. The causes of the north-south split of the kingdom of Israel are in 1 Kings 11–12. The defeat of the northern kingdom by the Assyrians is in 2 Kings 17, and the defeat of the southern kingdom by the Babylonians is in 2 Kings 24–25. The stories of the divided monarchies are in 1 Kings 12–2 Kings 25 and 2 Chronicles 10–36 (southern kingdom of Judah only).

The promise of God to David through the prophet Nathan for a perpetual throne is in 2 Samuel 7:1–17 (especially verse 16) and 1 Chronicles 17:1–15 (especially verse 14).

The Past Serves the Present. The dramas of David's life are found in 2 Samuel 11–24 (Bathsheba incident in 11:1–12:23). The transfer of power is in 1 Kings 1–2 and 1 Chronicles 23:1, Solomon's building of the temple is in 1 Kings 6, and the long addition of David's role in preparing the temple is in 1 Chronicles 22–29.

A Sneak Peek at the Political Map. My source for some of the previews of the monarchy in Genesis is Gary A. Rendsburg, "The Genesis of the Bible," http://jewishstudies.rutgers.edu/component/docman/doc_view/117-the -genesis-of-the-bible?Itemid=158. Also to a lesser extent, Jon D. Levenson, *The Death and Resurrection of the Beloved Son: The Transformation of Child Sacrifice in Judaism and Christianity* (Yale University Press, 1995).

The Tower of Babel story is in Genesis 11:1–9. The birth of Moab and Ammon to Lot's daughters is in Genesis 19:30–38. Esau sells his birthright to Jacob in Genesis 25:29–34. David's rule over Edom is mentioned in 2 Samuel 8:14, and Edom's rebellion in 1 Kings 11:14–22 and 2 Kings 8:20–24 (see also Genesis 27:39–40 for the preview).

Abraham's journey to Canaan, subsequent trek to Egypt to escape famine, and return home with riches are found in Genesis 11:31–12:20. Parallels to these episodes are in Genesis 46 (Jacob and his family go to Egypt to escape famine), Exodus 7:14–12:32 (plagues), and Exodus 12:31–36 (Moses is summoned to Pharaoh and the Israelites leave Egypt with riches). Abraham's "everlasting covenant" with God is in Genesis 17:7 and David's in 2 Samuel 7:16.

Playing Favorites with Little Brother. The "favored younger brother theme" is found in Genesis 4:1–16 (Abel over Cain), Genesis 21:8–21 (Isaac over Ishmael), Genesis 25:29–34 and 27:1–29 (Jacob over Esau), Genesis 37–50 (Joseph over his brothers), Exodus 7:7 (Moses over Aaron), 1 Samuel 16:1–13 (David over his brothers), and 1 Kings 1–2 (Solomon over Adonijah). Jon Levenson lays out these and other examples in *The Death and Resurrection of the Beloved Son.*

Adam, Who Art Thou? The story of Adam and Eve, which mirrors the story of Israel, is found in Genesis 2–3. The references to life as remaining in the land and death as exile are in Deuteronomy 30:11–20 and Ezekiel 37:1–14. Israel meaning "struggle with God" is given in Genesis 32:28.

The Exodus Story. The number of men delivered from Egypt is given in Numbers 26:51.

When Gods Fight. In the plague story, the reference to Aaron's staff swallowing up the staffs of Pharaoh's advisers is Exodus 7:8–13. The other incidents I mentioned of gods fighting are Exodus 7:14–25, 8:1–15, 10:21–29, and 12:29–32 (see also 12:12).

The days of creation where God splits the "deep" are days two and three and the story is found in Genesis 1:6–10. The idea of creation as the splitting of waters is also seen in Psalms 74:12–13, 77:16, and 104:7–9. Psalm 74:12–13 also refers to a sea monster Rahab and 89:9–10 mentions dragons (Tiamat of *Enuma Elish* was depicted as a monster). The description of the dividing of the Red Sea that echoes the creation story is found in Exodus 14:15 and 21.

What's with All the Water? Moses's basket is called *tevah* (ark) in Exodus 2:3.

CHAPTER 4—WHY DOESN'T GOD MAKE UP HIS MIND?

"If I Wanted to Tell You What to Do, I Would Have"—God. In Proverbs, the verses cited about "wealth" are 10:15, 18:11, 10:16, and 11:28.

When Biblical Writers Get Cranky. The "anti-wisdom" passages cited from Ecclesiastes are 1:18 and 7:16. Qohelet's dismal musings on death are in 1:11, and the positive nudge at the end of the book is 12:9–14.

"Don't Quote the Bible at Me, Please. I'm God."—God, to Job and His Friends. Job's ups and downs, and the challenge of the Adversary, are recounted in Job 1–2. His friends begin to convince Job that he deserves what he gets in chapter 4. An early example of Job protesting his innocence is in chapter 6. God's speech is in chapters 38–41 and his reprimand of Job's friends is in 42:7.

Is There More Than One God? (And, No This Isn't a Trick Question). The "mocking of idols" passages I refer to are in Isaiah 44:6–20, Jeremiah 10:1–16, and 1 Kings 18:16–46. Psalms that refer to Yahweh as one of many gods include 95:3, 96:4, 97:9, and 135:5. God saying "Let *us* make humanity . . ." is in Genesis 1:26.

God Seems Like a Regular Joe. Examples are taken from the story of Adam (Genesis 2–3), Noah (Genesis 6), the near sacrifice of Isaac (Genesis 22:1–19), and the golden calf incident (Exodus 32). Jesus sweating drops of blood is found in Luke 22:43–44.

God Lays Down the Law . . . Sort Of. Exodus 31:18 says that the tablets of stone were inscribed by the finger of God.

CHAPTER 5—JESUS IS BIGGER THAN THE BIBLE

Jesus Gets a Big Fat "F" in Bible. Jesus's interpretation of the burning bush story (Exodus 3:6) is found in Luke 20:27–40 (see also Matthew 22:23–33 and Mark 12:18–27).

Jesus Messes with the Bible. Matthew 16:15–17 is an instance in the Gospels where Jesus accepts the title of messiah (see also Mark 8:29–30 and Luke 9:20–22).

Jesus's interpretation of Psalm 110 is in Mark 12:35–37 (see also Matthew 22:41–46 and Luke 20:41–44). His interpretation of Psalm 82 is in John 10:34–36.

Jesus: Moses 2.0. Jesus's assertion that he has come to fulfill the law and the prophets is in Matthew 5:17–19, near the beginning of the Sermon on the Mount. Specific references made are to murder (5:21–26), adultery (5:27–30), divorce (5:31–32), solemn oaths (5:33–37), eye for an eye (5:38–42), and love your enemies (5:43–48). Following Jesus as taking priority over family obligations is seen in Matthew 8:21–22 (see also Luke 9:59–62) and 12:46–50 (see also Mark 3:31–35 and Luke 8:19–21).

Jesus Picks Fights. The episode of picking grain on the Sabbath is in Mark 2:23–28 (see also Matthew 12:1–8 and Luke 6:1–5), and the story of David Jesus mentions is in 1 Samuel 21:1–6. References to Old Testament prophets who put the practice of justice and righteousness over rote practice of sacrifice are Hosea 6:6, Amos 5:21–25, Isaiah 1:10–17, and Jeremiah 7:21–23.

The incident concerning dietary laws is found in Matthew 15:1–20 and Mark 7:1–23 (the dietary laws themselves are in Leviticus 11). The passage in Acts I mention where dietary laws seem to come up for the first time is Acts 10:1–33. Paul discusses them in Romans 14:1–15:6.

CHAPTER 6—NO ONE SAW THIS COMING

Good News! Our Leader Was Executed by the Romans! Come Join Us! Peter's rebuke of Jesus for saying he would die and rise from the dead, and Jesus calling Peter "Satan," is in Matthew 16:21–23. Paul's reference to a "new creation" in Christ is in 2 Corinthians 5:17. "Born from above" is in John 3:7 and "born again" in 1 Peter 1:23.

"It's All About Me."—Jesus (According to Luke and Matthew). Jesus's explanation that he is the goal and focus of the entire Old Testament is in Luke 24:36–49. Matthew's reference to the boy Jesus coming out of Egypt fulfilling the Old Testament is in Matthew 2:15–16, citing Hosea 11:1. The return home, prompted by the assurance that "those who were seeking the child's life are dead," is in Matthew 2:20 and mirrors God's words to Moses in Exodus 4:19.

Are We There Yet? The request of brothers James and John to sit at Jesus's right and left sides is in Mark 10:35–45 (see also Matthew 20:20–28).

Matthew's genealogy of Jesus that highlights the Davidic messiah bringing an end to the exile is in 1:1–17. (Luke's very different genealogy is in Luke 3:23–38.) The Beatitudes (the meek inherit the earth, etc.) are in Matthew 5:1–12. The Gospel references to John the Baptist being the "voice crying in the wilderness" are Matthew 3:3, Mark 1:1–3, Luke 3:4–6, and John 1:23. Matthew's final twist on ending the exile is in 28:16–20.

The general idea of Jesus "ending the exile" is articulated in N. T. Wright, *Jesus and the Victory of God* (Fortress, 1997).

Jesus, Savior of the ᵛ J̶e̶w̶s̶ World. Concerning Jesus's birth as a promise to deliver the Jews (ending the exile) in Luke's Gospel, Gabriel's announcement to Mary is in 1:26–38, Mary's song of praise to God is in 1:46–56 (which mirrors Hannah's song in 1 Samuel 2:1–10), Zechariah's praise is in 1:67–79, Simeon's prophecy is in 2:25–32 (citing Isaiah 49:6), and Anna's prophecy is in 2:36–38. Jesus's first public appearance, where messianic expectations begin to be redirected by Luke, is in 4:16–30. Jesus blasphemously forgives sins in 7:49.

God's Answer to a Question No One Was Asking. Paul mentions his run-in with Peter in Galatians 2:6–14. Paul's zeal for stopping the Jesus movement is recorded in Acts 8:1–3, and 9:1–31 mentions Paul's letter of permission from the high priest in Jerusalem to arrest Jewish followers of Jesus in Damascus and his experience of encountering the resurrected Christ. In Galatians 1:18 Paul mentions his three-year wait before returning to Jerusalem after his Damascus Road experience. Peter's resistance to Paul's attitude toward Gentiles is in Galatians 2:11–14.

The inclusion of the Gentiles as a "mystery" is in Ephesians 3:5–6. Paul's declaration that there is no longer "Jew or Greek" is in Romans 10:12 and Galatians 3:28. The "wall of hostility" between Jews and Gentiles that Christ's death and resurrection tore down is in Ephesians 2:14.

"Torah? Oh That. It Was Only Temporary."—God (As Told to Paul). Paul's reference to his former life of Torah obedience as "rubbish" in order to "gain Christ" is in Philippians 3:8. The abolishing of the law is in Ephesians 2:15.

Paul's interpretation of the Abraham story is in Romans 4, and his curious interpretation of Abraham's "faith" (Genesis 15:6) is in verse 3. Torah's late (and therefore non-central) arrival into the human drama is in Romans 5:20 (and Paul's view of the law here does not square with such passages as Psalm 119:105). Paul's reference to Torah as temporary guardian is in Galatians 4:1–7, and his unexpected handling of the Sarah and Hagar story (Genesis 16 and 21:8–21) is in Galatians 4:21–5:1.

"Why Don't You Just Go Castrate Yourself," and Other Spiritual Advice. The true mark that designates one as a person of God, faith working through love, is in Galatians 5:6. The circumcision command to Abraham is found in Genesis 17:9–14, and Paul's advice that his opponents castrate themselves is in Galatians 5:12.

The matter of whether or not to keep dietary laws (weaker and stronger brothers) is laid out in Romans 14:1–15:13.

CHAPTER 7—THE BIBLE, JUST AS IT IS

The word of God described as a two-edged sword is found in Hebrews 4:12.

The passage I refer to from the Talmud is in *Bava Metzia* 59b, and the passage from Torah alluded to there is in Deuteronomy 30:12 (see also 17:11).

Matthew is describing Jesus as Immanuel in Matthew 1:23.

Some Dates I Keep Referring To
(And a Few Others)

YOU CAN'T TALK about the Bible, especially the Bible and history (as in chapters 2 and 3), without bringing some dates into the picture. Here are the dates I refer to in the book, plus a few more that may help round out the picture. Some dates are approximate but close enough.

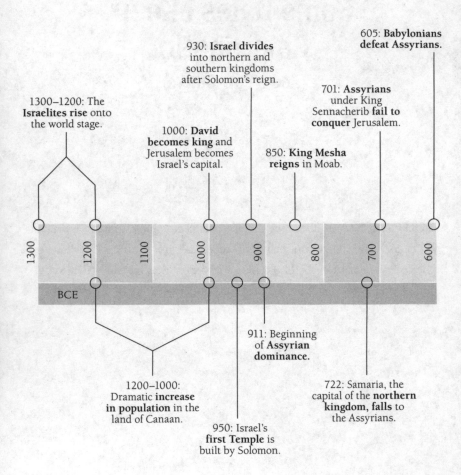

605: **Babylonians defeat Assyrians.**

930: **Israel divides** into northern and southern kingdoms after Solomon's reign.

701: **Assyrians** under King Sennacherib **fail to conquer** Jerusalem.

1300–1200: The **Israelites rise** onto the world stage.

1000: **David becomes king** and Jerusalem becomes Israel's capital.

850: **King Mesha reigns** in Moab.

BCE

911: Beginning of **Assyrian dominance.**

1200–1000: Dramatic **increase in population** in the land of Canaan.

722: Samaria, the capital of the **northern kingdom, falls** to the Assyrians.

950: Israel's **first Temple** is built by Solomon.

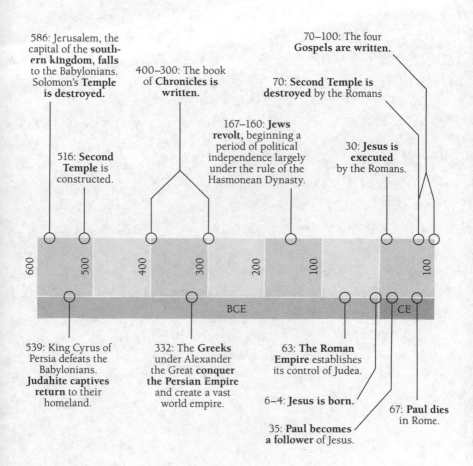

586: Jerusalem, the capital of the **southern kingdom, falls** to the Babylonians. Solomon's **Temple is destroyed.**

400–300: The book of **Chronicles is written.**

70–100: The four **Gospels are written.**

70: **Second Temple is destroyed** by the Romans

516: **Second Temple** is constructed.

167–160: **Jews revolt,** beginning a period of political independence largely under the rule of the Hasmonean Dynasty.

30: **Jesus is executed** by the Romans.

600 500 400 300 200 100 100

BCE CE

539: King Cyrus of Persia defeats the Babylonians. **Judahite captives return** to their homeland.

332: The **Greeks** under Alexander the Great **conquer the Persian Empire** and create a vast world empire.

63: **The Roman Empire** establishes its control of Judea.

6–4: **Jesus is born.**

35: **Paul becomes a follower** of Jesus.

67: **Paul dies** in Rome.

In Case You Don't Believe Me and Want to Read More

I'M KIDDING OF COURSE. Reading is good, and for those of you who want to do more reading about some of the things I covered in this book, here are some recommendations. Some of these books lean a bit toward the academic end of the spectrum, though they are not obscure. I've marked those with an asterisk.

Don't think that I agree with everything written in all these books, or that these authors would necessarily agree with me on everything. But it's all good. The broader we cast our net, the deeper we wind up owning our own thoughts—which is a muffed metaphor if I ever saw one, but I'm sure you get what I'm saying.

Baker, Sharon L. *Razing Hell: Rethinking Everything You've Been Taught About God's Wrath and Judgment*. Louisville, KY: Westminster John Knox, 2010.

*Batto, Bernard. *Slaying the Dragon: Mythmaking in the Biblical Tradition*. Louisville, KY: Westminster John Knox, 1992.

Bell, Rob. *Love Wins: A Book About Heaven, Hell, and the Fate of Every Person Who Ever Lived*. San Francisco: HarperOne, 2011.

Brettler, Marc Zvi, Peter Enns, and Daniel Harrington, SJ. *The Bible and the Believer: Reading the Bible Critically and Religiously*. Oxford: Oxford University Press, 2012.

*Brown, Raymond E., and Francis J. Moloney S.D.B. *An Introduction to the Gospel of John*. New York: Doubleday, 2003.

Brueggemann, Walter. *An Unsettling God: The Heart of the Hebrew Bible*. Minneapolis: Fortress Press, 2009.

*———. *Theology of the Old Testament: Testimony, Dispute, Advocacy*. Minneapolis: Fortress Press, 1997.

Burridge, Richard A. *Four Gospels, One Jesus? A Symbolic Reading*. Grand Rapids: Eerdmans, 2005.

*Campbell, Anthony F., and Mark A. O'Brien. *Unfolding the Deuteronomistic History: Origins, Upgrades, Present Text*. Minneapolis: Fortress Press, 2000.

*Clifford, Richard J. *Creation Accounts in the Ancient Near East and in the Bible*. Washington, DC: Catholic Biblical Association of America, 1994.

Dever, William G. *Who Were the Israelites and Where Did They Come From?* Grand Rapids: Eerdmans, 2006.

*Dillard, Raymond B. *2 Chronicles*. Nashville: Thomas Nelson, 1988.

*Dunn, James D. G. *The New Perspective on Paul*. Grand Rapids: Eerdmans, 2007.

Earl, Douglass S. *The Joshua Delusion: Rethinking Genocide in the Bible*. Eugene, OR: Cascade, 2011.

Enns, Peter, and Jared Byas. *Genesis for Normal People: A Guide to the Most Controversial, Misunderstood, and Abused Book of the Bible*. Colorado Springs: Patheos Press, 2012.

Enns, Peter. *Ecclesiastes*. Grand Rapids: Eerdmans, 2012.

———. *Inspiration and Incarnation: Evangelicals and the Problem of the Old Testament*. Grand Rapids: Baker, 2005.

———. *The Evolution of Adam: What the Bible Does and Doesn't Say About Human Origins*. Grand Rapids: Baker, 2012.

*Goldingay, John. *Theological Diversity and the Authority of the*
 ment. Grand Rapids: Eerdmans, 1987.

Gorman, Michael. *Reading Paul*. Eugene, OR: Cascade, 2008.

Hawk, L. Daniel. *Joshua in 3-D: A Commentary on Biblical Conquest and*
 Manifest Destiny. Eugene, OR: Cascade, 2011.

*Japhet, Sara. *The Ideology of the Book of Chronicles and Its Place in Biblical*
 Thought. Ann Arbor: American Oriental Society, 2009.

Jenkins, Philip. *Laying Down the Sword: Why We Can't Ignore the Bible's*
 Violent Verses. San Francisco: HarperOne, 2011.

Johnson, Luke Timothy. *The Real Jesus: The Misguided Quest for the*
 Historical Jesus and the Truth of the Traditional Gospels. San Francisco:
 HarperSanFrancisco, 1996.

Knight, Douglas A., and Amy-Jill Levine, *The Meaning of the Bible: What*
 the Jewish Scriptures and Christian Old Testament Can Teach Us. San
 Francisco: HarperOne, 2011.

Kugel, James L. *How to Read the Bible: A Guide to Scripture, Then and Now*.
 New York: Free Press, 2008.

*———. *Traditions of the Bible: A Guide to the Bible as It Was at the Start of*
 the Common Era. Cambridge, MA: Harvard University Press, 1998.

Levenson, Jon D. *Creation and the Persistence of Evil: The Jewish Drama of*
 Divine Omnipotence. Princeton, NJ: Princeton University Press, 1994.

———. *The Death and Resurrection of the Beloved Son: The Transformation*
 of Child Sacrifice in Judaism and Christianity. New Haven, CT: Yale
 University Press, 1995.

———. *Sinai and Zion: An Entry into the Jewish Bible*. San Francisco:
 HarperSanFrancisco, 1987.

Levine, Amy-Jill, and Marc Zvi Brettler. *The Jewish Annotated New Testa-*
 ment. Oxford: Oxford University Press, 2011.

*Miller, J. M., and J. H. Hayes. *A History of Ancient Israel and Judah*.
 Second edition. Louisville, KY: Westminster John Knox, 2006.

*Moore, Megan Bishop, and Brad E. Kell. *Biblical History and Israel's Past:*

ᴈing Study of the Bible and History. Grand Rapids: Eerdmans,

, Steve. Paul and Scripture: Studying the New Testament Use of the
Old Testament. Grand Rapids: Baker, 2010.

ackle, Keith F. The Synoptic Gospels: An Introduction. Louisville, KY:
Westminster John Knox, 2001.

Perriman, Andrew. Heaven and Hell in Narrative Perspective. CreateSpace
Independent Publishing Platform, 2012.

Rendsburg, Gary A. "The Genesis of the Bible." Accessed June 19,
2014. http://jewishstudies.rutgers.edu/component/docman/
doc_view/117-the-genesis-of-the-bible?Itemid=158.

*Seibert, Eric. Disturbing Divine Behavior: Troubling Old Testament Images
of God. Minneapolis: Fortress Press, 2009.

*Smith, Mark S. The Memoirs of God: History, Memory, and the Experience
of the Divine in Ancient Israel. Minneapolis: Fortress Press, 2004.

*Sparks, Kenton L. "Gospel as Conquest: Mosaic Typology in Matthew
28:16–20." Catholic Bible Quarterly 68 (2006): 651–663.

*———. The Mystery of Israel's Origins: An Introduction and Proposals.
Oxford: Oxford University Press, 2014.

*Stager, Lawrence E. "Forging and Identity: The Emergence of Ancient
Israel," in The Oxford History of the Biblical World, ed. Michael D.
Coogan. Oxford: Oxford University Press, 1998.

Stark, Thomas. The Human Faces of God: What Scripture Reveals When It
Gets God Wrong (and Why Inerrancy Tries to Hide It). Eugene, OR: Wipf
and Stock, 2010.

*Thomas, Heath A., Jeremy Evans, and Paul Copan, eds. Holy War in
the Bible: Christian Morality and an Old Testament Problem. Downers
Grove, IL: InterVarsity Press, 2013.

Williamson, H. G. M. 1 and 2 Chronicles. Grand Rapids: Eerdmans, 1982.

Wright, N. T. How God Became King: The Forgotten Story of the Gospels.
San Francisco: HarperOne, 2012.

*————. *Jesus and the Victory of God*. Minneapolis: Fortress Press, 1997.

————. *Paul in Fresh Perspective*. Minneapolis: Fortress Press, 2005.

————. *Simply Jesus: A New Vision of Who He Was, What He Did, and Why It Matters*. San Francisco: HarperOne, 2011.

Zehr, Paul M. *Biblical Criticism in the Life of the Church*. Harrisonburg, VA: Herald, 1986.

Acknowledgments

I'D LIKE TO ACKNOWLEDGE MYSELF. Writing is hard, and I'm wiped.

In addition I'd like to acknowledge:

Apple Computers and the Microsoft Corporation for devising a machine that can let me keep Facebook and my email open while I'm working and, at the same time, monitor my spelling as I type and keep me from inventing my own random rules of grammar.

MLB.TV for making it possible for me to have a little window open on my computer screen so I could watch the Yankees while staring blankly at my book-in-progress because I have absolutely nothing worthwhile to say right now.

The almighty, omniscient Internet (and Verizon FIOS) for having every single conceivable piece of information—some of it accurate—ready and waiting for me the instant I need it. And for YouTube.

David Vinson, J. R. Daniel Kirk, Bradley C. Gregory, Sam Boyd, David Williams, Nathan Mastnjak, Lise Porter, Elizabeth Enns Petters, Eric Flett, Dwight Peterson, A. J. Levine, Anthony Le Donne, Christopher Keith, Steve Bohannon, Kent Sparks, John Franke, and several other not-to-be-named friends, currently in the Evangelical Witness Protection Program, for reading portions of the various drafts of this book, and giving sincere, perceptive, and invaluable feedback. You made this book much better.

Having said that, I still hold you all fully responsible for the mistakes you missed. I was counting on you.

Westminster Theological Seminary, which opened many windows and doors for me in the early years, some of which I have since needed to close. Some.

My Harvard professors, James L. Kugel and Jon D. Levenson, for being willing and gracious enough to teach a goy how to understand their Bible by modeling what it means to read it carefully, respectfully, and with both eyes open to a past much wider and deeper than I had realized.

My editor at HarperOne, Mickey Maudlin, and his amazing team, for their professionalism and guidance, for often knowing what I wanted to say better than I was saying it, for keeping me from various embarrassments, and for their enthusiasm for this book from day one.

My agent at Creative Trust, Kathy Helmers, for being with me since the beginning when I first emailed *Hey, you don't know me, but there's this book I want to write,* for being able to read my mind, for helping me craft the vision with wisdom, intuition, and skill, and for liking dogs and baseball more than books.

My dogs, Gizmo and Miley, for giving me a writing break every fifteen minutes because they absolutely needed to go out right now and chase an errant molecule of something and then dash back in for a treat. My cat Marmalade, for climbing on my keybo^]/r9875gggggggg, and for my other cat Snowy whose girth makes him too gravity challenged to even think about it and so just sits there.

My students at Eastern University, who are trying to follow Jesus, ask big questions, figure out life, get a job after they graduate, and yet, with all this going on, *still* somehow manage to get my many and unreasonable assignments in on time (by which I mean pretty late). You also remind me why I do all this.

St. Matthew's Episcopal Church for telling us about Jesus every Sunday with sincerity and depth in twelve minutes or less, showing us Jesus the rest of the time, and for giving rest and a cup of cold water to many travelers, including me.

My wife, Sue (grammar goddess, finder of missing words, and verb tense corrector), read the entire manuscript near the final stages and caught many mistakes. My daughter Lizz Enns Petters ("I've been able to spell better than my dad and beat him at Scrabble since I was eight") read portions early on. My oldest, Erich ("I can't imagine ever writing a book, but I'd be happy to critique yours"), and youngest, Sophia ("When I try to tell my friends what you do for a living I don't know what to say"), were also, as always, supportive. Truth is pretty much every word I write is with all of you in mind. Please don't put me in a home.

God, for my health, the time and opportunity to put my thoughts in writing, and a house with a desk to do it in. I am learning still, as the Prayer Book says, that "It is right, and a good and joyful thing, always and everywhere, to give thanks to you, Father Almighty, Creator of Heaven and Earth," and not take these blessings for granted.